our selves, our bodies, our hearts—and in the process, to reconnect directly with the accumulated effects of trauma, even when this requires facing one's ghosts."

—**Steve Balt**, MD, MS, Editor in Chief
of *The Carlat Psychiatry Report*

"*The Trusting Heart* is a richly-textured and multi-layered exploration of the intimate personal healing journey of the author. Michael Aanavi finds a way to connect the acutely intra-personal nightmare of trauma and addiction to the universal embrace of the transpersonal and the legacy of the multi-generational. This is truly a gift to all who suffer, that is to each of us in our own way."

—**Steven Hickman**, PsyD, Director of
UCSD Center for Mindfulness

"With this book, Dr. Michael Aanavi has made a major original contribution to the voluminous literature on addiction and recovery. Aanavi integrates anecdote and theory, the personal, cultural, ancestral and archetypal in an illuminating and healing way. He writes of addiction as "medicine" for unbearable inner pain, and of healing through finding true "medicine" in his own inner world, in the processes of shifting and transforming "deeply embedded, consciously inaccessible [psychosomatic] narratives of illness." His method of treatment, as presented in his writing, is fundamentally to "be" from his own self experience and self knowledge, and thus to illuminate for other sufferers the hope and trust that they, too, can find their own individual pathways. I recommend this book very highly."

—**Steven Joseph**, MD, physician, psychiatrist
and Jungian analyst, member and training analyst,
C. G. Jung Institute of San Francisco

THE TRUSTING HEART

Addiction, Recovery, and Intergenerational Trauma

MICHAEL AANAVI, PhD

Foreword by Eduardo Duran, PhD

CHIRON PUBLICATIONS

2012
CHIRON PUBLICATIONS
P.O. Box 68, Wilmette, Illinois 60091
www.chironpublications.com

Book and cover design: William Jens Jensen

LIBRARY OF CONGRESS CATALOGING-IN-PUBLICATION DATA

Aanavi, Michael.
  The trusting heart : addiction, recovery, and intergenerational
trauma / by Michael Aanavi ; foreword by Eduardo Duran.
      p. cm.
  Includes bibliographical references and index.
  ISBN 978-1-888602-56-2 (alk. paper)
  1. Substance abuse. 2. Addicts--Rehabilitation. 3.
Intergenerational relations. I. Title.
  HV4998.A16 2012
  362.29--dc23
                                  2012032351

Contents

For my parents, and theirs.
For my teachers, and theirs.
With gratitude, *l'dor vador.*

FOREWORD

I have worked for three decades with people who are suffering soul wounding, and the symptoms that come from this trauma. There are many approaches, and at times it appears as if there is a flavor of the month in treating symptoms of historical trauma especially when it comes to addictions. Some of the approaches focus on finding the source of trauma; others focus on the addiction itself.

Aanavi's story takes us into the belly of the beast in an exploration of the soul's wounding and stands eye to eye with the demons in an honest attempt to make a different relationship with these entities...Aanavi hones in on the entity of heroin, which is the one spirit visitor that has given him the gift of insight during this lifetime. That said, he gives us the insight into his awareness and lets us understand that this type of awareness is costly and it requires additional sacrifice of both flesh and spirit. The insight I get from this type of intense process is from the Promethean metaphor of stealing fire and in the process we become singed...i.e., the price of fire (insight) ain't cheap and the gods still demand a high price from us.

It is with deep gratitude that I acknowledge Mikey's process of going into the underworld to bring us this treasure of wisdom and insight. The treasure is the understanding that if we want to heal from the spiritual chokehold called addiction, we must go into the hell realms that include the wounding of our ancestors as they also scream for healing as they traverse the spirit world in whatever form that may take. Mikey has traversed those realms and in so doing has healed the ancestors he talks about in this book...he has done more than that in having the courage to put this in print. He has given us the medicine and path that we may also heal and in so doing has lowered the cost of our insight because he has paid some of the entry fee on our behalf.

I truly hope that all of you who read this story can do so with an open heart and allow the heart to take you into the hell realms you may need to go for your individuation process. It's a difficult journey and is the journey for spirit warriors. Mikey has given you a map...at some point the map will get you to a dead end. Do not stop, keep going and you will be on your own without a map...this is your own journey and you can only take his journey to a certain point because that is his journey. As the *Tibetan Book of the Dead* teaches us...at this point you will see a goddess with a corpse in one hand and a skull full of blood in the other, do not be afraid.

Eduardo Duran, PhD
Bozeman, Montana
November, 2011

"Seek out that particular mental attribute which makes you feel most deeply and vitally alive, along with which comes the inner voice which says, 'This is the real me,' and when you have found that attitude, follow it."
—WILLIAM JAMES

THE TRUSTING HEART

"What if we discover that our present way of life is irreconcilable with our vocation to become fully human?" —PAULO FREIRE

I am a psychologist, an acupuncturist, a heroin addict in recovery, and a Jew from New York raised in rural Hawaii. I have a host of identities, a complex of stories about who I am—stories that nourish each other, dance with one another, run together in my work and in my daily life.

I've had wonderful teachers—academic, clinical, and spiritual. It's been my great fortune to have had (perhaps a bit too much) formal education, and to have learned even more from patients, colleagues, and friends. Yet the most important thing I've learned (and am learning, daily) is how to attend to my lived experience—my stories, my culture, my intuition. Having grown up in this fragmented, manic society, amidst violence, intergenerational trauma, and family alcoholism, the hardest—and most valuable—thing for me has been the process of learning to trust not just that which is gathered from external sources, validated by society, but that which I feel in my bones, touch with my heart, and see in my dreams.

Carl Jung spoke of *pistis*, the trusting heart. He said that this fundamental capacity for trust is the precursor to faith—that without this essential quality, faith in something greater, faith in one's own process, faith in the wholeness of the psyche is impossible. For me, *pistis* involves my ability to trust my own subjectivity, my own felt sense, regardless of whether it jibes with what's externally acceptable or valid, regardless of the outcome. I first lost touch with this core sense of integrity because of trauma—not just my own trauma, but also the trauma of those who came before me: the injuries of my ancestors carried in my family, in the deep layers of my psyche, and in my body.

A new kind of connection with my own experience began more than twenty years ago, with the commitment to simply be here and accept the discomfort of life as a human being—though at the time I had no idea that was the decision I was making. I was finally willing to do anything necessary to stop using heroin, and embedded in that willingness was a choice beyond any concept of what it would bring. Early on in my recovery, in residential treatment at Phoenix House in New York, I sat in groups and was for the first time aware of the traumatic rupture of my inner world, although at the time I had neither language for it nor the ability to frame my experience. I was checked out, disconnected from everything around and within me. As emotional content arose in myself and others, I would lose myself in daydreams and stories or by simply spacing out; I was so skilled at this, from years of practice in childhood, that I could actively participate in groups without others knowing I wasn't really there.

Of course, a lot of us (perhaps even most of us) live in this way—checked out, elsewhere. There's a connection, in my experience, between the societal phenomenon of disconnection, the process of addiction, and the effects of personal and transpersonal trauma. As many others have discussed, traumatic disconnection is both psychological and somatic— but even past this, at the core of the psycho-somatic experience of trauma, there is something that is not solely personal, but rather is transpersonal, intergenerational. Like the story of the blind men describing the elephant, I've found that Jungian psychology, Chinese medicine, and a number of other perspectives and practices each shed their own light on this phenomenon, but that the whole is much bigger, and at the same time, much smaller: it's personal, subjective, experiential.

There's much to elaborate on here. In what follows, I write further about my experience over the past twenty-plus years, both as a person in recovery and as a clinician. This book, *The Trusting Heart*, is about this exploration, this process, this commitment to that which is both profoundly personal and remarkably vast: to telling the stories of one's experience, to the integrity of one's felt truth, to following one's energetic thread wherever it might lead.

DANNY

"Say I'm leaving this Babylon.
It will not be too long.
It will not be too long now."
—BAD BRAINS

I was clean for about three weeks before I went into treatment. It wasn't easy—I was subletting an apartment on 13th Street and Avenue B, one flight up from the apartment of a heroin dealer, in a building next door to a shooting gallery. I could get high without putting my shoes on.

Danny showed up at my door one day during that three weeks and dragged me to treatment—like he did for so many others. He had conned me out of $700 in a drug deal two years before but was now in recovery; he heard I was trying to get clean and tracked me down.

I remember seeing his face in the fish-eye of the door, being at once furious and vengeful and exhausted, thinking I should hurt him in some way for his violation of my trust, but knowing that I wouldn't—in truth, I was happy to see him. This time, my umpteenth attempt at staying clean, I had hopped a bus to my mother's house in Massachusetts, spent a few days being dopesick and pilfering her Valium to take the edge off, hopped a bus back to Manhattan and the dismal flat where I lived in terror—now clean, but afraid to go outside for fear of running into the dealer or someone else I knew, for fear of slipping back into my habit. I was effectively a shut-in, and Danny's arrival brought rage, but also hope, and relief.

It turned out he'd been in long-term treatment in Arizona for a year and a half, and had only recently returned to New York. Danny's mother and my father were old friends, and the news of my hopeless habit and vain attempts to break it had traveled quickly from my father to Danny's mother to Danny—and had triggered a true urgency on Danny's part. I later learned he was HIV positive and had already started to become ill, an almost-certain death sentence in those days—the late '80s and early '90s—when treatment for AIDS meant AZT and wishful thinking.

Like so many others, I lost a lot of friends in that era—not just from AIDS, but from suicides, overdoses, car wrecks, and so on. Knowing he was sick, Danny had returned from Arizona with a sense of desperation, with a sense of his own mortality, with a clear acceptance of his own fate and a mission to prevent others from suffering the same. So he showed up—for me and many others. He used every dope fiend trick he had up his sleeve (and he was a consummate dope fiend) to con or drag us into treatment: he convinced me that if I went to treatment he'd pay me the money he owed me when I got out.

Soon after I was born, my father brought me to visit Lena, Danny's mother, at Westbeth, a housing community for artists in the West Village, where Danny and Lena lived with Danny's adoptive father, Arthur. Lena remained fond of telling the story of that visit: how I'd gurgled, motionless, in a bassinet; how three-year-old Danny had complained, "Mom, it doesn't *do* anything." She was fond, too, of pointing out that in my adulthood I still didn't really do anything—which was true, in a substance-induced way, when Danny and I met again at college. I'd had only intermittent contact with him since our early childhoods; I have vague memories of fishing from a rowboat in the Hudson with Danny and our respective fathers. But when we met again as adults, our connection was immediate, largely revolving around drugs and music. Despite the three-year difference in age, we were at about the same point in school. Danny was far more advanced in drug use, however. He was, by that time, shooting heroin and cocaine in large quantities, which is what led him to steal from everyone he could, quickly crash and burn, and wind up in long-term treatment in Tucson.

Back in New York, Danny helped me get into treatment; he helped me flush a pound of mushrooms down the toilet before I went in (I wanted to keep them to sell when I got out, a notion he persuaded me wasn't all that bright), and he helped me move into my new sublet on 109th and Broadway when I got out. He sent others to treatment in Massachusetts, Arizona, New York, sometimes paying for plane fares and detoxification with credit cards he knew he wouldn't live long enough to have to pay off. And he got sicker. I visited him in AIDS wards and pneumonia wards and, finally, at St. Vincent's, in a private room where he'd been brought to die.

He and I had become brothers. Already almost family because our parents had been so close, we became closer as he helped guide me away from active addiction, as we grappled with the harshness of the therapeutic community model of treatment we'd both endured, and as I sat with him and his failing body and watched him face his mortality. At the end, he was no longer there: ravaged by CMV, entangled in his hospital bed sheets, he looked up at me. And although he knew me, he didn't know where he was: "Whose house am I in, Michael Aanavi?" he asked me. "Your house, Danny," I told him. I didn't know what else to say. I couldn't bear to tell him the truth.

The next day he died.

We had two memorials for Danny. At the official, grown-up memorial, people in suits stood around an Upper East Side apartment, solemn and mournful, and I and others read poetry and spoke about

Danny and witnessed Lena's devastation—she had lost Arthur years before to Hodgkin's disease, and now her only child. It helped a bit to imagine Danny's smirk, to imagine what his reaction would have been: cynical, sardonic, calling this one a schmuck and that one a mamaluke, secretly loving every minute of it. And at the unofficial memorial, in a room somewhere in the bowels of Westbeth, a dozen or so of us who had known him, loved him, had contentious, bittersweet friendships with him, sat around while the Cro-Mags (for whom Danny had been an early drummer) and Bad Brains (whom he'd managed for a time) each played a set. I thought about starting the kind of old school punk-rock riot Danny would have loved, throwing some chairs, jumping into a pit, but instead just sat in my chair—apparently, chronically, still not doing anything.

Of course, Danny never did pay me the $700 he owed me.

Danny was the finest anti-hero I ever knew, and he embodied for me what it means to have integrity— to lovingly, emphatically follow what feels right, regardless of what others say, regardless of the outcome. From the streets on which he was raised came the ideal of being a stand-up guy—a man who kept his mouth shut, who took his lumps without complaint, who knew the order of things. In treatment those street ideas were confronted and ultimately had to be let go, but for Danny I think the notion of being a stand-up guy was simply transformed, redefined: for him, being stand-up meant accepting his reality; it meant showing up for those he loved; it meant breaking rules and crossing boundaries, not in order to get over or get what he wanted, but in service of life and the possibility of change.

Recovery

*"Life is trouble. Only death is not. To be alive
is to undo your belt and look for trouble."*
— Zorba the Greek

For me, recovery is not about management of a chronic disease; it is a continual process of recovering something so fundamental, so ineffable, it's almost impossible to know it except by its absence.

It's not recovery *from*, it's recovery *of*.

When I was little I knew what I wanted, knew what felt right to me. I wouldn't go along with others to go fishing, for example, if I didn't want to—if I was drawing or thinking or involved in some other project or priority of my own. I wasn't oppositional, didn't grandstand or throw tantrums; I was simply clear about who I was. Or, at least, this is the case according to my mother, who is admittedly biased.

Evidently, somewhere between this quiet childhood confidence and my adolescent willingness to participate in any dumbass, self-destructive activity in which others were engaged—and to invent a few dumbass self-destructive activities all on my own—something happened. But specific events aside, the point is this: there was a time when I lived in connection to myself, and however it came about, a time when I became disconnected.

That's the case for many, if not most of us, and it doesn't necessarily involve trauma, or addiction, or drama of any kind. It's just the case; we lose a sense of who we are. And we do so in a culture that supports disconnection, dissociation. But for me there's more to it than this societal backdrop: there's a direct link between trauma (both personal and transgenerational), disconnection from one's self, and addiction—and there's a link between reconnection and recovery. Or, more succinctly, reconnection *is* recovery.

During graduate school I had the privilege of training with Dr. Eduardo Duran at the Native American Health Center in Oakland, where Dr. Duran placed equal emphasis on psychotherapy and traditional healing practices. I recall a Dineh medicine man who came to the clinic regularly to meet with patients, all of whom were of Native American descent, but many of whom had grown up in urban settings and had little if any connection with the traditional practices of their ancestors. The medicine man would set out certain implements as he met with patients—an altar, feathers, other implements—and more than once during a session (which we as therapists often attended) a patient would say, "But I didn't grow up with this stuff! I don't know these things!" The medicine man would typically grin and reply, "That's okay, they know you."

Recovery is like that: a process of rediscovering a place within yourself that you know, even if you don't know you know it—or, rather, rediscovering a way of being in the world, a way that knows you, viscerally, intuitively, in the deepest reaches of psyche and bone.

Prayer

"It is when we pray truly that we really are."
—Thomas Merton

"The function of prayer is not to influence God, but rather to change the nature of the one who prays."
—Søren Kierkegaard

Despite relating the intimate details of my experience of addiction, trauma, and recovery, in some ways it feels almost too personal to talk about prayer; it's one of those hidden things. But this sense that something so much an essential part of my experience and my recovery should be hidden suggests to me that there's an element of shame at play—a feeling that I am fundamentally flawed, which I carry from both personal experience and intergenerational transmission: a feeling that I am simply *wrong*. In Jungian terms, this is an experience of shadow, of that part of the psyche that is all the unwanted, intolerable aspects of experience, both personal and transpersonal—and an experience of the way in which the feeling of shame, of badness, of wrongness is an important doorway to connection with the shadowy aspects of my inner life.

If just the thought of discussing prayer brings all of this to the forefront, eliciting such strong feelings, then delving further into it is an important act of connection. To paraphrase Pema Chödrön, lean into the sharp points...

As a child I prayed from a place of desperation. Without a religious or spiritual upbringing, I did it spontaneously, with a natural desire to connect with something during a time of great need. Yet within this childish prayer, this plea to please make all my pain go away, addressed to whatever being I imagined, within this desperate desire for relief and escape lay the very root of my addiction: the process by which I sought over and over again to make everything stop. My prayer of desperation ultimately transformed into a spiritual relationship with weed, with alcohol, with heroin; in some sense my prayers were indeed answered in the way in which that intention—to make it all stop—was eventually fulfilled, at least for a while. In the interim, though, I took what felt like a lack of response to my early prayer as evidence of prayer being useless and ineffective, as confirmation of the indifference of whatever or whoever I thought wasn't listening.

Early on in recovery I was told that prayer would help me stay clean. My terror of relapse far outweighed the resentment I felt because of seemingly unanswered prayers, so I prayed, and somehow it helped. This prayer, though, was less an act of faith than it was an act of trust in other recovering people, an acknowledgment of how little I knew about how to function as a human being, how little I knew about how to be alive without running. And in many ways my early recovery prayer was much like my childhood prayer: it was born of fear and the need for relief, of desperation and the fantasy that something would magically make everything bad go away. Even in prayer, I was disconnecting, disavowing, feeding the shadow rather than finding ways for it to nourish me.

As the saying goes, prayer does not require belief, only the willingness to suspend disbelief. It does, though, require intention. But if the intention of my prayer is to flee, to be elsewhere, the result, in my experience, is more shame, more disconnection—a reprisal of the addiction-trauma dynamic.

It took a different experience of prayer—in Judaism and in the Indigenous world—for me to begin to slough off my personal and transpersonal shame. Only then was I able to begin to emerge from the ways in which my escapist prayer had further manifested my experience of trauma and disconnection. For me now, prayer is about neither worship nor supplication; rather it is a practice of being with whatever is present, of recognizing in the moment my tendency to shift away from my experience, of working with personal and collective shadow by welcoming whatever is unwelcome, whatever feels shameful—including, sometimes, prayer itself. In this form, the power of the intention to connect has been profound in transforming my experience of what Jewish mystics refer to as *galut*: exile, disconnection. But when I pray I'm neither an addict nor a Jew nor a Buddhist—nor, in those moments when I'm in the flow of it, even really myself. I'm simply a heart, and if I can through prayer find ways to truly be in the moment, then I'm at last, fleetingly, a trusting heart.

MY NAME IS MICHAEL

"where there is nothing to believe in,
when I am desperate
and see no future for me,
then my life
is a lover's breathing
on embers of a dream"
—JIMMY SANTIAGO BACA

It's a Jewish custom to name children for a deceased family member, and in that tradition I'm named Michael, for my paternal grandfather, who died long before I was born. My father and his father also never knew their grandfathers, and in a way there's something disrupted, even traumatic about being the third generation in the male line of my family not to have known our paternal grandfathers. But although I've always had a connection to him as his namesake, my grandfather Michael is someone I'd just as soon not have known.

Michael was at best erratic, at worst brutal and cruel. By all accounts brilliant (although never formally educated), he worked a variety of jobs—in grocery stores or whatever else was available—but was more often unemployed. I'm told he worked as an informant for Senator Joseph McCarthy, was photographed for a newspaper covering his face in shame on his way to testify, but this is one of those family legends I'd just as soon believe wasn't true. I've often felt his presence—through my father, in the way in which Michael made my father who he is, and my father made me who I am; in my father's ambivalence toward me that mirrored his ambivalence toward his father, for whom he named me; and in my bones, in the shadows, in a feeling of unrest, a sense of dread that I know is not just mine, but also his.

Michael was the oldest of several children—I'm not sure how many, perhaps seven or eight. I know of Robert, my great uncle, a retired physical education teacher, as well as my great uncles Larry and Max, the former of whom lived in St. Louis, the latter of whom had been in prison in Ossining for murdering his wife. There were others: a sister or two. But I've never known their names.

Their parents emigrated in 1898, from where, I'm not sure, but it's understood in the family that their lineage was Sepharadi, not Ashkenazi. They settled in the Lower East Side of New York, where all their children were born, and where Michael's mother, my great grandmother, died of influenza in 1914. Michael's father was badly injured in a factory accident. Unable to care for his children, he did what was done in those days; he placed them all in an orphanage—all, that is, except Michael, the oldest, who was sixteen and joined the army during World War I.

From that point Michael was distant, separate from his siblings, and certainly never really known to my father, his son. What I know of Michael is through my father, not just from his descriptions, though I've heard a few, nor just through stories of Michael's brutality, though I've heard those as well, but rather through what's not said—through my father's dark silences, during which I imagined his father (and his father before him), during which I felt their absence and saw myself reflected in the depth of my father's sadness and loss and pain.

From my father I know that although his father never drank he was often violent, toward my father and especially toward my father's mother, whom Michael never married. In their common-law marriage Michael often brought home prostitutes and other women—along with his shame and his rage.

Michael loved handball, a love he shared with my Uncle Joey, my father's older brother, but never with my father, a decidedly non-athletic child. Michael also respected education, and despite his chaotic personality he was a passionate, learned Jew who, poor as they were, insisted my father go to a *yeshiva* in the Bronx where they lived.

When my father was fourteen, his mother died. A few months later—perhaps of a broken heart, perhaps of unbearable guilt, perhaps simply because he no longer had an external target for his self-hatred and rage—Michael died as well. He was buried in a veterans cemetery somewhere on Long Island. My father, the only person to attend the funeral, received his father's folded flag.

I suspect Michael was bipolar. And I know, given his internal chaos, his own harsh history, and his basic humanity that he's deserving of compassion. But it's hard for me not to think of him harshly, even brutally. This brutality, though, this legacy of his, is the very ancestral transmission I seek to transform. I am not only his namesake; I am his blood, his essence, inherited through stories and relationships, and I share his brutality—toward him, toward myself. I understand some of the reasons he was the way he was; others I will never know. For some things I can easily forgive him, others less so. But in all things, rather than retaliating or disavowing, it is essential that I find a way to love, even to forgive, this fragmented, disturbed man who was responsible for so much horror and suffering—and whose name I carry.

I feel him lingering—his shame, his self-hatred, his deprivation. I feel the legacy he inherited: Jews brutalized for centuries in Europe and elsewhere, immigrant Jews carrying the European shadow to America, the loss and rupture of his life and his family. I feel his horror at what he enacted, his guilt, his self-recrimination—and I feel the shame he felt in his inability to stop. I know this part of him intimately. I knew it well in my own addiction, still see it in myself.

This is the legacy of trauma, its intergenerational transmission—this experience of brutality, not just directly, but in the gaps, in the still silent spaces in which self-attack emerges, in which compassion is at best an afterthought. In these spaces, still, my first thought is to disconnect, to say that I am not him, to disown any connection with him and his heritage, to hold myself clean and clear. But I am him, and we share our unrest as well as our name. I am named for him, not to honor him, but rather to allow him— and those who came before him—to live, through me, long enough to find rest.

BODY AS RECOVERY

"When the opponent expands, I contract.
When he contracts, I expand.
And when there is an opportunity, I do not hit.
It hits all by itself."
— BRUCE LEE, in *Enter the Dragon*

As with many who have experienced trauma, simply having a body has always been a challenge for me—and in fact much of my addiction was about seeking every possible means to avoid embodiment. But trauma aside, my constitution is such that my body always carries an element of shadow—it's a source of shame, it's what trips me up when I'm not paying attention, it's where I can most easily become disconnected.

My body tells me when I'm on or off track, sometimes by generating pain or illness, other times when I simply feel disconnected from my bodily experience. If I'm not connected with my body's integrity, if something feels wrong but I'm not paying attention, if I'm being dishonest with myself or compromising my sense of what feels right in some fundamental way, the first place in which this shows up is in somatic disconnection. It is also the growing edge of my experience, a constant process of integration, and in this sense embodiment is itself a path of recovery.

In treatment at Phoenix House a lot of emphasis was placed on paying attention to when something "flips your belly"—when something feels right or wrong, viscerally. At first it was a struggle for me to grasp this concept, for like most addicts I had ignored that type of awareness for so long that I'd become deaf to it. For a long time I simply felt shut down, as though someone had poured wet cement into my torso and it had hardened there. And I was terrified, too, of what might emerge if I opened again to that place of truth. Finally, one of the counselors—I think it was Cornelius Bracey, who passed away from lung cancer in the '90s—said to me, "Listen, motherfucker, did you ever get ripped off buying dope on the street?"

"Yeah."

"And when you gave the man your money, did you know in your gut that it wasn't dope, that you were gonna get beat?"

"Yeah."

"Do you remember that feeling in your belly, the one that told you this shit ain't right?"

"Yeah."

"Well that's the motherfuckin' feeling, and I want you to pay attention, and any time you feel that motherfuckin' feeling, no matter where, I want you to speak the fuck up about it, even if you don't know why the fuck it's happening."

I did speak up. And speaking up about that sensation in early recovery—probably more than anyone really wanted to hear—is, to a large degree, probably why I'm still clean. But that process, that embodied awareness, is about more than relapse; it's more than simply connecting with my feelings. As a dedicated practice, as a form of mindfulness, as a commitment to remaining open to my experience, it connects me with the thread of my own truth.

If something doesn't feel right, it's difficult for me to stay connected to the most fundamental aspects of my experience, to remain in my body without checking out. And even if I can't change the situation, simply staying connected to the uncomfortable feeling—in my belly, or in whatever somatic way I might experience it—is, though hard, essential, because when I willfully ignore that perception, I've lost my rudder, and it lands me squarely in that place of disconnection that becomes a kind of living death.

Toward the conclusion of my Jungian analysis, my analyst and I spent a lot of time talking about how I might continue my analytic work on my own—in particular, about ways in which I might continue delving into and integrating shadow. When I asked him for his parting guidance in a nutshell, knowing me well, he said, "Let your body be your guide." And truly, difficult as it sometimes is, much as I would still sometimes prefer to check out, I can always trust my body's guidance.

TRANSPERSONAL DEPRIVATION

"Longing is the core of mystery.
Longing itself brings the cure.
The only rule is, Suffer the pain.

Your desire must be disciplined,
and what you want to happen
in time, sacrificed."

—RUMI

I'm often aware of a feeling of deprivation, of a sense that I need something outside myself to soothe a deep want or need. I'm aware of it when I feel the need to purchase something without which I think I'll perish. I feel it when I eat just a bit beyond satisfaction, not because of appetite but because of a desire to check out. And I know its presence when I feel the deep longing that for me comes with (and without) relationships, the longing for connection with another whom I fantasize will meet the depth of my need and magically make it go away.

I've known this presence my whole life, but for many years only subtly, through the behavior it induced—through all the machinations in which I engaged to avoid feeling it. I could not be aware of this presence, could not tolerate it, could not begin to contain it long enough to lend it consciousness. I grew up in a world, in a culture, in a family in which such things were not voiced, in which the pervasive hunger of the soul was met with variants on my grandmother's well-intentioned greeting, "Come in, you must be starving," in which alcohol and food and television and every other stopgap measure was easily available, but not awareness. And, of course, there was heroin—there was no better relief from the unbearable tension I didn't even know I had.

When I first began to meditate in the Buddhist tradition, in New York in the early 1990s, I would sit for long periods overwhelmed by anxiety, lust, wild thoughts of every kind, and by a feeling of emptiness, by the sensation of a pit in my torso so deep and profound I had no words for it—could barely tolerate it. In treatment I had been introduced to my body's wisdom, and I now knew this pit of deprivation for what it was—the root of my craving, not just for heroin but for anything that might make the emptiness seem bearable for just a moment. Not the void of which Buddhist masters spoke, this void of mine made me feel as if I was going to die if I couldn't fill it.

Slowly I learned to sit through it and recognize the ways in which my meditative ruminations and fantasies helped distract me from the reality of this thing that I wanted more than anything to avoid. But the real fantasy never came true: the fantasy that if I sat through it, that if I let myself experience it, that if

I learned to be with it—and that if I went to enough therapy—somehow it would transform, resolve, go away. The feeling of deprivation remained, and still remains, perhaps triggered less frequently than it once was but no less severe when triggered, no less dire, no less urgent. My response to it now is different than it was, and more often than not I simply know it for what it is, but there is something about that void that is timeless, terrifying—that says to me when it arises, "I am here, I am unbearable, I am forever."

A few years ago an image came to me, a fantasy that would not leave me alone—an image of a little girl in the distant past, dead of starvation, doll-like, with hollowed eyes and tattered dress. In the darkness I saw her in a doorway, hand outstretched, face sunken; I was aware of her presence both visually and through the physical experience of starvation and abandonment, and through the experience of the pit in my abdomen. I was not simply aware of her pain, her fear, her deep hunger—I was those experiences. I was her. Her hunger was in me, and I could not feed her, could not sufficiently assuage the depth of her longing, could not comfort her fear nor change her fate. And I knew in my heart that this was an ancestral image.

Although perhaps this image was literally an ancestral "ghost" (the lingering, haunting spirit of an ancestor who died unresolved), or perhaps simply the symbolic residue of historical trauma emerging from the deep layers of the psyche, the real truth of this image lies simply in my experience. And my experience is that my ancestors emerge in me, live through me; that the deep deprivation of which I've long been aware is not simply the result of a disruption in my early childhood care. For despite later chaos, my parents were quite present in my early childhood, quite aware, quite caring. This lifelong experience of deprivation is neither explained by mainstream psychological theories nor by theories of addiction; it is explained by what I know intuitively. It is explained by the reality that I am linked deeply, in body and psyche, to those who came before.

This transpersonal, historical, ancestral awareness has been remarkable in allowing me to sit with my void in a different way. I remind myself that it's not simply about me, nor about a wound I received in my infancy, but about them, my ancestors, about my connection with a larger process of resolution, and by giving this deprivation both context and meaning I find myself able to bear my experience in a different way; I find I am able to be kinder, both to myself, and to her, in all her forms.

Archetypal Narratives and Defects of Character

"We cannot change anything until we accept it. Condemnation does not liberate, it oppresses."

—C. G. Jung

I often have the sense that I am living within a story, a narrative in which events and ideas unfold and in which I too am unfolding. It feels as if the roots of this process go deeper than I could ever know, into realms that are by their very nature unknowable, except perhaps in dream. I wonder whether this is the experience to which Jung referred when he spoke of the archetypal realm, the deep layer of the psyche that emerges in myth, in symbol. Jung said that archetypes don't happen in us but rather that we happen in them. And the sense I have of my life as a story evolving just outside my awareness is what I imagine he might have meant.

There are times when I see clearly the tenuousness, the ephemerality of whatever story is present, and there are times when I am completely in the grip of my narrative, when I fully believe my own stories—what Jungians would call being caught in a complex. Among the most difficult and pervasive of these is the story of nothing ever quite being good enough—the core belief that nothing is entirely acceptable, that everything and everyone (including me) deserves critique, that all will never be sufficiently well.

In the recovery world the term "character defects" is often used to describe this kind of state with which addicts, and humans in general, struggle. These are the parts of us—call them wounds, or complexes, or schemas—that require ongoing maintenance, constant vigilance, and perhaps a relationship with something larger than ego-consciousness to keep them from taking over and dictating our actions. For many, though, the term "defect of character" is problematic because it feels pejorative, pathologizing. For me, this language is difficult not simply because I find it insufficiently compassionate but because it perpetuates in me the idea that I am fundamentally defective. It doesn't help me in seeing my own dynamics simply as unfolding stories.

It is not difficult to justify my narrative of inadequacy and criticism. It makes sense: in trauma, in chaos, survival dictates hypervigilance; one must be on guard, perpetually observant, especially for anything that might be a threat. And even beyond my personal experience, a sense of threat is present in my ancestral reality—in Jews' historical experience, lingering in the subtle realms of my psyche: Romans,

Cossacks, Nazis. There is, in this intergenerational transmission, always a story about someone coming—with horses and swords, with guns, cattle cars, and gas chambers—a story in which my vigilance is absolutely warranted. But the legitimacy of my cultural and personal experience, of my reflexive response—my story of self-protection—is the very thing that convinces me of the inescapable truth of my own stories.

My *taijiquan* teacher, Dr. Benjamin Tong, has for many years repeated the maxim "nothing fixed," presenting a Daoist point of view in which nothing can be static, in which nothing *should* be static, especially not identity nor self-perception. From this perspective, illness and dysfunction are by nature rooted in rigidity and fixedness. And for me, the construct of character defect as a "truth" rather than as a story—however justifiable, however deeply rooted—only increases identification with my stories as fixed phenomena, as illness, rather than narratives with the potential to be let go.

Ezra Bayda, Zen teacher and author, suggests a wonderful inquiry, "What is your most believed thought?" For me this enquiry has a way of poking a sharp stick into the ingrained stories that so often have me in their grip. Also, Pema Chödrön's dictum, "Drop the story line and feel the underlying energy," seems to exhort me not to buy into my endless narratives. Sayings such as these are remarkably effective for me; the systems of thought they encapsulate make me, in the moment, just a tiny bit less susceptible to a complex—or, in recovery language, to my character defects running wild.

Further, recognizing the *nature* of these stories feels valuable; their archetypal and historical origins, hopeful. For this awareness brings with it an opportunity to alter my sense of being flawed and defective by beginning subtly to change my relationship to my stories, from captive character to discerning reader. In viewing character defects not as parts of a static identity but rather as stories susceptible to inquiry, to movement, to fluidity, there lies a chance of truly changing my narrative.

CHINESE MEDICINE, ARCHETYPAL MEDICINE

"Another world is not only possible, she is on her way. On a quiet day, I can hear her breathing."

—ARUNDHATI ROY

Like most who seek out spiritual practice and deep healing, my own exploration has been fueled by illness, pain, and suffering, and my introduction to Chinese medicine was no exception. During my second year of graduate school in clinical psychology I began to experience severe gastrointestinal symptoms, and was soon diagnosed with ulcerative colitis and placed on anti-inflammatory medication to control flare-ups. Pharmaceuticals were somewhat helpful in reducing the more extreme symptoms (in particular, severe bleeding), but they left other symptoms, as well as the underlying condition, unresolved. Then only in my late twenties, I was reluctant to remain on medication for the remainder of my life—especially given the unknown long-term side-effects of these medications.

Having had some exposure to Chinese medicine through Sat Chuen Hon, my former *qigong* teacher in New York, I had the sense that this might be a useful alternative to allopathic medicine. Asking around, I found my way to an acupuncturist of good repute, a naturopathic doctor. His integrative approach was somewhat helpful, but I intuitively knew that what I needed was a more traditional approach to Chinese herbal medicine, so for several years I continued to explore and seek out practitioners, until with great fortune (and by referral from Dr. Benjamin Tong) I found my way to Dr. Joseph Chi Ng. Almost immediately Dr. Ng ameliorated my symptoms, and over time my ulcerative colitis was fully healed and I was able to taper off pharmaceuticals entirely.

Dr. Ng is, in my experience, both a remarkably kind human being and a highly skilled practitioner of classical Chinese medicine. But being "highly skilled" in this context means a great deal more than simply being knowledgeable about pulse diagnosis, the application of acupuncture, and the properties of herbs. According to Master Jeffrey Yuen, eighty-eighth generation Daoist priest of the Jade Purity lineage (and himself an extraordinary teacher and practitioner of Chinese medicine), the practitioner's own self-cultivation is key to the practice of classical Chinese medicine; it is this cultivation that allows the medicine to reach levels of depth and transformation that go beyond any ideas of a "cure." Interestingly, this idea is quite similar to Jung's notion that the analyst's own analysis is the cornerstone of their training, that deepening one's own relationship with the unconscious, engaging fully in what Jung called "individuation," is what truly enables an analyst to facilitate this process for others.

A practicing Buddhist for many years, Dr. Ng is praised often by his patients not only for his unique skill with acupuncture needles, medicinal herbs, and other methods of Chinese medicine, but also for his self-cultivation, compassion, and the ways in which he integrates illustrative storytelling in his clinical work. Along with the physical treatment he administers, Dr. Ng typically shares anecdotes with patients—about himself, about something that happened to him that morning, about fictitious people he once knew—and these anecdotes (or, more accurately, healing stories or allegories) both reflect Dr. Ng's quirky character and resonate at deep levels in concert with the physical aspects of his medicine.

Like many, when I first heard Dr. Ng's stories, I thought he was just eccentric—even, perhaps, a bit cracked. I had no idea why he was telling me about his friend, or the engine of his car, or about a fictional patient he'd seen that morning. I continued to return for treatment simply because of the immediate effectiveness of his herbal medicine, but eventually began to have breakthrough moments in which I suddenly recognized—hours or even days later—the nature and importance of something he had told me. And even when I didn't completely understand what he'd said, I did notice the deep effect—the resonance of these stories—and also the ways in which my experience of my body and my symptoms themselves began to shift. Even after I'd been Dr. Ng's patient (and, later, his student) for years, it was still often difficult to know exactly why he was telling me what he was telling me, but in my experience cognitive understanding isn't the point of this truly classical form of psychotherapeutic Chinese medicine. Nor is it really necessary. Reminiscent, perhaps, of the work of the great hypnotherapist Milton Erickson, this approach touches undifferentiated places within me that I don't know are there until I come to be aware of them in hindsight, after some shift brought about by a subtle and artful combination of stories and herbs.

During my Jungian analysis—while my ulcerative colitis was still active—an image arose in an active imagination of a claw penetrating my bowels: dark, gnarled, simultaneously avian and reptilian. This was a central symbol for me, an image that bore within it the story of that illness—a story ultimately related to trauma, to my carrying in the deepest recesses of my body a kind of viciousness that had been activated in me, that had become self-attacking, tearing at itself like the autoimmune disorder it was. It has now been years since I've experienced that image, since I've been aware of the presence of that claw; indeed, that particular story seems to have been fully told.

Jung described archetypes as having two poles, one spiritual or symbolic—emergent in dreams and the creative process—the other somatic: the embodiment of a narrative that emerges from a place so deep and undifferentiated it's neither body nor mind but rather is expressed in both. In a sense Jung was talking about a true mind-body medicine, a medicine accessible both symbolically and somatically; his understanding has been explored and expanded upon by a variety of post-Jungians through somatic psychotherapy, homeopathy, and other methods. But Jung's own understanding, I think, speaks more directly to what Chinese medicine has done for centuries in its capacity to access seemingly inaccessible realms: to shift deeply embedded, consciously inaccessible narratives of illness.

There are, of course, many practitioners of classical Chinese medicine—along with other forms of what might be considered energetic or vibrational medicine—who work in these subtle ways, accessing depth with their various methods. Some of those who come to mind are Lori Eve Dechar, author of *Five Spirits*, and Robert Levine, a remarkable practitioner in Berkeley with a deep mastery of pulse diagnosis. Given Master Jeffrey Yuen's emphasis on self-cultivation, it is evident to me that whatever the type of intervention, in many ways Chinese medicine is a kind of personal and transpersonal transmission that registers in the subtle and undifferentiated realms of body, energy, psyche. In some way, through the manipulation of needles, through knowing what story to tell at the right time, and through a variety of other methods, the classical Chinese tradition is a truly (and wholly) archetypal medicine with the profound capacity to shift narratives as they emerge in both body and mind, and in places deeper than either.

My Grandfather, Nobility, and Sour Cream

"Whatever you end up doing, love it. The way you loved the projection booth when you were a little squirt."
—Alfredo in *Cinema Paradiso*

My mother used to tell me that we were descended from Russian princes, that I was royalty. I don't know where she got this idea—what with her blue-collar Queens upbringing and the fact that neither of her parents had roots in Russia. Her mother's family came from Riga, in Latvia, by way of England, and her father's from Ostroda in Danzig, which was sometimes Polish, sometimes German, sometimes something else, depending on who'd conquered the area that week. And then there's the obvious dissonance between Jews and Russian nobility—Cossacks, intellectuals, revolutionaries.

My maternal grandfather, Saul, was a real *mensch*—but a baffling, enigmatic sort of *mensch*. He fixed things for everyone; he was the person to whom everyone came with emergencies, problems, clogged plumbing, and busted radios. He always helped—sometimes intrusively so—and typically responded to whatever came his way with his own little snippet of dharma: "Don't worry. Everything's gonna be all right."

A projectionist by trade, he grew up in an era of cinema in which men wore trench coats and fedoras and women looked hard and smoked constantly. As a young man, he left his parents' farm in upstate New York to "seek his fortune" and meandered from job to job, fixing things, boxing a bit, and eventually winding up in his chosen profession. A true farm boy, he worked hard, had conservative ideas about life and gender, and got into everybody's business whether they liked it or not. My grandmother apologized for him—a lot. "It's okay," she'd say, "he means well," immediately followed by, "Sit down, I'll make you something to eat."

Grandpa lived in a fantasy world in which there was a right way to do things and people acted as they ought—a world in which marriages lasted and love was eternal, like in the movies. After my parents split up, he'd often say to me, "So, when are your parents getting back together?" I'd reply, "Never, I hope."

My father and grandfather never got along, never understood each other. I think the conflict started when my mother ran off to Hawaii with my dad, got married, and got pregnant (with me)—in that order, but unforgiveable nonetheless. My grandparents had never met my father, had no idea who he was, and certainly had never heard such a strange—and to their ears not Jewish—last name. To make matters worse, my father was an academic, and contrary to stereotypes of Jews being the "people of the book," being concerned with knowledge for its own sake, my practical, working-class grandparents had no use for an art historian. To them, the purpose of education was stability, security—fine if one were to become a physician, attorney, dentist, something safe, lucrative, and with status. But my grandfather, a lifelong, staunch union man, reader of the *Daily News,* eater of meals on the clock at 7, 12, and 6, neither related to nor respected a man who didn't work with his hands, and who had an education but no profession. Grandpa was baffled and, I think, insecure in the face of anything not fitting just-so into his world, and this made him afraid, and sometimes even unkind.

Every year or two my grandparents would come from New York to visit us in Hawaii. They'd stay a couple of weeks, typically showing up with a suitcase full of bagels, kosher salami, and other delicacies that were unavailable on the Big Island. Grandpa loved Hawaii, but mainly because he simply loved warmth, and sun; he would have spent as much time in Florida as he could, except that my grandmother hated the place. When visiting us, he'd find things to fix around the house, he'd argue with my mother, but most often he'd sit outside, in a folding beach chair, with the sun on his face.

At home in Bayside my grandparents kept kosher—kosher meat, separate dishes for meat and dairy, clearing out everything for Passover. Meals were either *fleischig* or *milchig*, and when *milchig* were intensely *milchig*: butter, cream cheese, and the ubiquitous sour cream, my grandfather's favorite, reminiscent of fresh dairy from his youth on the family farm. These dairy meals often revolved around *lukshen* and cheese: egg noodles drenched in butter, cream cheese, cottage cheese.

Outside the home, though, all rules were off, and in restaurants my grandfather would rush to order his favorite thing: pork chops. My father, knowing well his father-in-law's proclivities, wanting for once to please this man with whom he'd had a decade-long standoff, found a recipe for pork chops in sour cream sauce—my grandfather's two favorites, trumped only, perhaps, by duck. That year, when my grandparents came for their pilgrimage—I must have been eleven—my father made that recipe for their first night with us, as a welcoming meal. We sat down to eat, and my father proudly began to serve, thinking, perhaps, that my grandfather would be pleased, even touched.

My grandfather wouldn't eat it because it was milk and meat together. A kosher faux pas. Despite the fact that he would happily have eaten the (anything but kosher) pork chops on their own, he balked at flesh slathered in creamy white sauce; it was simply too much for him to handle, too great a strain on his sense of rightness. And it also probably felt to him like a jab in the face from his egghead son-in-law, who had attended orthodox *yeshiva* and who certainly knew what was kosher and what wasn't. A massive argument ensued, culminating in my grandfather shouting, "I don't have to take this shit from you!" and storming off. My grandmother, I'm sure, said, "It's okay, he means well."

I ate the pork chops in sour cream sauce. They were really good.

My fondest memories of my grandfather are of time I spent with him in the basement of my grandparents' duplex in Bayside, Queens. Down there, amidst tools, the smell of camphored clothes, and my grandmother's laundry area, my grandfather's projector lived, with a folding screen and file cabinets full of film. He'd show me movie after movie: cartoons, when I was very young, although after his death I learned that at least one of the cabinets was full of "blue" movies—classic black and white porn. He read to me before bed, too, on those occasions on which I stayed over—my favorite story being *A Gift Bear for the King*. I would ask him to read it again and again, until finally he recorded himself reading it on his reel-to-reel and simply sat with me while he played it over and over until I fell asleep. But there was something special about the cartoons—about sharing with him his private space in the basement, watching his peasant, thick-fingered hands deftly thread the projector, sitting with him while we watched together, helping him rewind the films by hand, turning the crank as the film flipped from one reel to the other, as the end slapped against itself making that telltale sound of cinematic ending.

I sometimes wish I'd made the film *Cinema Paradiso*. Giuseppe Tornatore must have had a grandfather like mine.

After his first stroke—likely from the combination of inactivity and sour cream, which eventually killed him—my grandfather's speech was a bit limited. My conversations with him had never been deep or lengthy, but now when I visited I simply sat next to him and watched TV. Sometimes we'd go out for a bit, for pizza or to put gas in the Buick Regal he hardly drove anymore, and I'd watch his hand fumble and shake when he pulled out his wallet to pay the gas station attendant. No more fixing things for him; no more talking about the state of the world and how everyone would be better off if they stayed married.

I was in college when his health started to fail. It was the mid 1980s, and the crack "epidemic" was in full force, figuring prominently in almost every news show. We'd watch the news together, my grandfather and I, and he'd turn to me and say, haltingly, "So, you smoke crack?" assuming, I suppose, that everyone my age did so—especially hoodlumish, black leather clad, chain smoking kids like me. I'd say, "No, Grandpa, I don't smoke crack," and he'd sit back, apparently reassured—but he'd ask again at the next newscast. And the next.

I'd wait for my grandparents to go to bed, then go down into the basement—the place in which my grandfather and I had shared so much time, so many movies, such connection—and I'd get high on whatever I'd brought with me: pot in high school, or sometimes speed; later, heroin. But no Grandpa, I don't smoke crack.

My grandfather died of his final stroke while I was in Phoenix House. My mother had told her extended family that I'd left New York for LA to work on a movie; meanwhile, in treatment on West 74th Street, I talked about how I'd been unable to function in the film industry because in heroin withdrawal my hands had been too shaky for me to work as a camera assistant—I couldn't pull focus smoothly. I was given a pass for the day to attend my grandfather's funeral, somewhere in Long Island where they keep the dead, and I kept up the family fiction that I'd been in LA, that I was a good grandson who had taken leave from work and flown in to say goodbye.

"No, we are not descended of Russian royalty," I'd reply to my mother's fantasy of nobility, to her need to be something more than her blue-collar Bayside origins, something more than *lukshen* and cheese,

Buicks, and the Daily News. "Mom, we're not even Russian," I'd tell her, even while understanding full well her desire to leave her background behind.

But me? Me, I'm anything but noble.

Depression, Hope, and Time

"Sisters of despair, why didn't I kneel lower
to receive you, surrender myself more loosely
into your flowing hair. We waste our sufferings.
We stare into that boring endurance beyond them
looking for their end. But they're nothing more
than our winter trees, our dark evergreen, one
of the seasons in our secret years—
    not just a season,
but a place, a settlement, a camp, soil, a home."
                                —Rainer Maria Rilke

The thing about depression is, it's forever. Or, at least, it feels that way. Inside that state, time has no meaning, and the knowledge that it will at some point pass is at best arbitrary and theoretical, at worst a distant fantasy that brings with it false hope—and hope, whether false or not, only makes things worse.

I first heard the expression "this, too, shall pass" as a teenager, from Steve, my mother's boyfriend at the time. It was 1979 or thereabouts, and Steve had a few years previously returned from a tour with the Marines in Vietnam, where he'd nearly lost both his legs to a land mine. Although he never talked about his experience—at least, not to me—he certainly knew about difficult times and whether or not they might pass. I recall vividly Steve's badly scarred legs and the deep black marks within which shrapnel was still lodged; I recall, too, his kindness, his vain attempts to intercede when my mother, drunk and furious at my father and her father, even more furious at me because I reminded her of them and of the wreckage of her own life, would lash out at me with her self-contempt and vitriol.

In response, I withdrew, shut down: became sullen, static, and chronically sad. I withdrew into books, and into the forest in which we lived, into the fantasy worlds of the page, of my own psyche, of the green paths and muddy roads of Kokee. I lost interest in things, became dull, unconcerned, and eventually, in boarding school, obese—depression, incessant bong hits, isolation, and unlimited dining hall food will do that.

On one of my summer visits home I must have been particularly depressed, or perhaps had a particularly horrible row with my mother: Steve took me aside, or maybe he took me for a hike, and he told me the story of a king who sent his wisest advisors to the desert for ten years, charging them with distilling the world's great wisdom. At the end of the ten years, they returned to court and the king asked for their results. The chief among the advisors said, simply, "Your majesty, this, too, shall pass."

I remember appreciating Steve's concern, at a time when any concern, any real attention from anyone meant everything—it meant survival. And I remember, cynical teenager that I was, thinking this story was trite drivel. But mostly I remember thinking it was just plain wrong—the horror of depression (and, perhaps, of adolescence) being the feeling that nothing will ever pass.

What I remember most from the years of my mother's onslaught is the deep sense of shame I felt—the sense that I was somehow simply bad, and that if I could be better, if I could be different, if I could be someone else, I would be safe, and happy, and loved. Perhaps an aspect of my mother's sense of herself, transmitted to me in the way in which these things are passed from one generation to the next, shame is certainly at the root of my depression and disconnection, and when in these states I am inordinately susceptible to the shame-based wish for things to be different. From that realm, seeking relief in the desire for bad things to pass only takes me out of myself, out of my experience, and into that desire to be elsewhere, to be otherwise—deeper into a self-imposed shame that becomes truly crippling.

Jung once described a particularly psychotic patient as being "on the moon." Marie-Louise von Franz, his student, corrected him, asking if he didn't in fact mean that the patient *believed* she was on the moon. Jung, always more concerned with the legitimacy of subjective experience than with any external reality, replied, "No. She's on the moon."

Depression comes and goes, and I have indeed sought cures, resolution, fixes of all kinds for this painful state—not just for the despair that arises, but also for the lingering sense of disconnection from all that is truly alive in both my inner and outer world, the flatness that leaves me with the sense of being a ghost in my own flesh. But the idea, the fantasy that this will pass simply isn't true, at least while I'm in it—in it, hope itself is the enemy; it is a delusion that propels me away from the exquisite, hard truth of the present.

Pema Chödrön has spoken more eloquently than I have of the ways in which hope disconnects, the ways in which it sets up a dynamic of always striving to be elsewhere. It's natural, of course, when in a painful, seemingly hopeless state, to want relief, to want a cure. But the truth of it is, for me anyway, in depression, hope doesn't bring relief, and the cure—if there is such a thing—comes in welcoming such states as teacher, friend, home. To paraphrase Ezra Bayda, difficulties are not obstacles; they themselves are the path. And when in places of deep sorrow and ghostly disconnection, the notion that this too shall pass, however true it might be, has a way of ushering me to the end of the path rather than allowing me to simply be on it.

ADDICTION AS MEDICINE

*"Nothing in this world is a gift. Whatever must
be learned must be learned the hard way."*
— CARLOS CASTANEDA

The first time I did heroin, I knew I was home. I was with two friends in a dump of an apartment in Alphabet City; they had tried heroin for the first time the week before, and wanted to do it again, so I went along—gladly. Several hours later, after lying on a mattress, scratching, nodding, throwing up, I stumbled home, up Avenue B, already wanting more.

I was unequipped to deal with my psychic pain in any way other than simply shutting it down—by any means available. Heroin became that means, at least for a while, and I loved it for the way in which it made bearable the unbearable. Other drugs had done a fair job of deadening, disconnecting, but only fair; what I sought was a kind of psychic death, a living stasis, and when I found heroin, I knew I'd finally come to the solution I desired: a circuit breaker, an off switch. This was the drug, the feeling, the state of sacred dissociation I'd been seeking in every other drug, in every other experience.

And there was, indeed, something sacred, something holy in my relationship with heroin—something deeper than the way in which it protected me from feeling what I couldn't allow myself to feel, something more substantive than the idea of symptomatic self-medication—for me it was, in the truest sense of the word, *medicine*.

Dr. Eduardo Duran has written of the Spirit of Alcohol, and of the ways in which addiction is a relationship with a spiritual being—a relationship that ultimately becomes distorted and inappropriate. This is entirely consistent with my experience, both in active addiction and in recovery, but in my experience there's a tendency in mainstream recovery and in the psychological and medical communities to think of these substances—these beings—as by definition problematic, by nature destructive. This is not only misguided; it's damaging in the sense that it becomes a way of disavowing the experience of addiction, of projecting shadow onto the substance rather than allowing even the awful parts of the relationship with it to propel one into a process of wholeness. In this pathologizing of addiction, the possibility of addiction becoming *medicine* is lost.

Christina Grof has written at length of the ways in which addiction is, even in its potential for destruction, actually a movement toward wholeness rather than simply a destructive, negative act; I highly recommend her book *Thirst for Wholeness* for elaboration on that phenomenon, that profound possibility. And I recommend Dr. Duran's work as well, both personal and clinical. But what I want to underscore is the way in which heroin brought me face to face not just with my own mortality, not just with my own flawed and self-destructive drives, but with the existential necessity of choice, the question, as Camus described it, of whether or not to live. I had, for many years, both before and during my addiction to heroin, sought *not to live*—in a very real physiological sense, and in the psychic death of my constant disconnection. I recall, at the age of twenty, knowing I was not going to live to see twenty-five, and accepting this as a reality borne of my choices. But by the age of twenty-two, in the depths of my relationship with the opiate spirit, I knew that I had to find a way to emerge from the living death of heroin's maternal embrace.

The gift of my initiation through heroin was not just the way in which it medicated me, not just the way in which it allowed me to survive by disconnecting me from my own inner world; the true gift was the way in which heroin brought me into the depths of my own psyche—both bodily and spiritually—and refused to allow me to live in that state of ambivalence any longer. My relationship with that entity was first protective, then excruciatingly painful, then near deadly, and the deep phenomenon of that relationship continues to be embedded in my recovery in a constant process of choosing to be alive, of confronting those parts of my psyche that still wish for deadened states, of making the choice on a daily basis of not just whether or not to use, but of whether or not to face my own shadow, whether or not to disconnect, whether or not to have a life rather than a living death.

It's not at all my intent to glorify or revel in heroin addiction, nor to suggest that anyone purposefully seek out its depths. I don't think this can happen consciously or purposefully, anyway, but only through the necessity of seeking balm for seemingly unbearable pain. But once engaged, once the relationship with that entity is entered, there is a luring into greater and greater depths, into an absolute confrontation with psyche that, like any initiatory process, requires the reality of facing life and death and of dealing with the very real consequences of being called to that realm. I have lost far too many friends to make light of that reality, to be in any way blithe about it, to spiritualize it in a superficial way; rather, it's important to me to call attention to the spiritual reality of confrontation with this shadow, and the true existential crisis that entails.

Recovery is not easy, nor should it be. In leaving behind aspects of my relationship with that spirit, it is not as if I have left behind either the experience of it or its outcome; it is not some hateful substance which evilly seduced me and which now I must detest, but rather it is a relationship that brought me to the razor's edge of choice, to the process of waking up to recovery, which is not about getting better from an illness but rather continuing to find *medicine* in my own inner world. I do not claim to understand the machinations, the underpinnings of how these things work, nor do I claim particular knowledge of this spiritual being—I can only describe my experience of it, and of the way in which it has allowed me to choose, moment to moment, imperfectly, whether or not to be alive. In this sense it has been the greatest of medicines, and I am deeply grateful.

Trauma, Self-Sabotage, and the Red Thread

"When you do something, you should burn yourself up completely, like a good bonfire, leaving no trace of yourself."
—Shunryu Suzuki-roshi

Much of my path of recovery from trauma has been a continual process of connecting with my own energy, my own directionality; as my analyst put it, it's been (and continues to be) about following the red thread of my psyche. As a child, in order to maintain at least the illusion of psychic safety, I sought not just psychological and somatic disconnection, but the severing of a deeper, underlying layer—I found a kind of energetic disconnection, a rupture of that fundamental sense of what is and is not me, and the process of reconnecting with this elusive quality has driven much of my inner and outer work in recovery.

There's an oft-told story of Michelangelo's famous sculpture of David: someone was awestruck at the artist's ability to create such a masterpiece and asked how Michelangelo could possibly create such a sculpture; Michelangelo replied that he simply chipped away everything that was not David.

Recovery is like this, and the post-traumatic process of chipping away everything that is not me—in order to follow my own subtle energy, my own red thread—has been, and continues to be, quite circuitous, often not resulting in what might be perceived as success in the form of worldly outcomes that would yield a sense of satisfaction and stability. Many times I've dismantled my life, changed course—I've undone relationships, left jobs, and done things in a variety of ways that look very much like what might be referred to as self-sabotage. And in some ways I've indeed acted out of my fears—of surpassing those who came before, of the vulnerability of success, of the risk inherent in forward movement. There's a way, too, in which my visceral, inherited sense that the Cossacks or Romans will be coming at any moment sets up the core belief that for me to do well, to be happy, to actually have a life is somehow dangerous, and untenably vulnerable.

In his book *The Inner World of Trauma*, Jungian analyst Donald Kalsched has written of what he calls archetypal defenses of the self—of the role of what he refers to as daemonic self attack in the psyche's protective mechanism—and this perspective has been quite valuable in coming to understand the ways in which I sometimes undo myself. A more esoteric explanation of this phenomenon, the Daoist understanding (according to Liu Ming) that this kind of unsettledness is often a manifestation of ghostly, unresolved ancestors has also been a valuable perspective.

But there's another side to this phenomenon that often looks like self-sabotage, meandering, unsettledness. There is the red thread: the ongoing choice to find, or rather restore, a sense of integrity with my own process by following what feels right to me, no matter the temporal outcome. This is a necessary practice of integrity borne of the experience, in childhood and in addiction, of having sacrificed that very integrity in service of the hope of protection and safety.

In making the choice to follow what feels right to me, in choosing the restoration of the energetic process that was severed in trauma, it's sometimes been necessary to give up the illusion of safety and security—the very thing my psyche often tells me I most want and need. This is not to say that safety and security aren't valuable and appropriate, but rather that when faced with the choice between successful outcome and following what feels right—in my heart, in the pit of my gut—it's been essential for me to develop the practice of following the latter. This means, of course, a certain degree of unpredictability, an acceptance of what Dr. Benjamin Tong has often called, from a Daoist/existentialist perspective, the radical contingency of life as a human being.

This is not recovery in the sense of repair of wounds or cure of illness; rather it is the recovery found in a willingness to err, in a letting go of outcome—the recovery of an energetic integrity through the commitment to following that red thread, uncomfortable and terrifying as that might sometimes be. Jung spoke of the process of circumambulating the psyche, suggesting that the path of individuation is by no means linear, but rather looping and coiling in inexplicable ways, and that surrender to its vagaries is necessary, essential for wholeness. For me, this surrender has required that on many occasions I let go of everything other than what feels necessary, what feels true, even when that seems irrational, foolhardy, self-destructive. And, frankly, in hindsight some of the choices I've made might have been mistakes indeed, and certainly have caused me difficulty and pain. But it's only been through surrendering to my own subjectivity, mistaken or not—without making excuses for those mistakes—that it's been possible for me to develop a connection with my energetic thread, to begin at last to chip away everything that is not me. In this sense self-sabotage doesn't matter, nor does outcome; what matters, for me, is a redefinition of success in terms of a relationship with my own energetic integrity—success defined in terms of being true to my own directionality—rather than in terms of worldly outcome. For better or worse, the only way in which I can know that directionality is by feeling my way through, step by step, until that very process, that elusive connection once upon a time ruptured by trauma, feels like home again.

Reyna, My Grandmother

"All the dreams you show up in are not your own."
— Gil Scott-Heron

My maternal grandmother was from the old country: Brooklyn. Her older brother and sister were born in England, where the family lived for a few years on their way to America from Riga, in what's now Latvia, and my grandmother was the first of the family born in the U.S., which I think had some significance for her, and for them—I remember her being politically active, a lifelong staunch Republican, in contradistinction to her husband, my grandfather, who was steadfastly labor affiliated, and whose sisters had done editorial work for the *Daily Worker*.

There was always some dissonance between my grandparents, I think. They loved each other, and were dutiful in their marriage, but my grandmother came from more money, and perhaps a bit more class, than my blue-collar farm-boy grandfather, and she had very different ideas about how to live, dress, and of course vote. Her family owned a resort in Moodus, Connecticut, sort of a mini-Catskills known for its Jewish resorts. They would spend summers there and the rest of the year in their brownstone in Brooklyn. Her father, I think, had other endeavors, other properties, but the family's life was really rooted in Moodus—and even after the hotel burned down, and after her parents passed away, the lives of my grandmother and her siblings still revolved around spending summers in Connecticut, where they'd built cottages on the land that had once been the family business.

My grandmother gave me baths in the sink in that cottage in Moodus, when I was small enough to be bathed in a sink. My grandfather, the handiest of the husbands, kept things in order. He allowed me to steer when he drove the old broken-down pickup to the dump, and sat me on his lap on the riding mower when cutting the vast lawn. My grandmother, never one for sitting still, cleaned and cooked and cleaned some more. She spent time with her sisters, chatting as they all cooked in the communal kitchen or sat in folding chairs in the sun (though she herself never sat long)—I remember other family members and guests lounging and sunbathing, but never my slender, active grandmother.

When I was in boarding school in Connecticut I'd often spend a week or two with my grandparents in Moodus—at the end of the school year, before heading back to Hawaii for the summer, or in the weeks before Labor Day, on my way back to school. Summer in Moodus was always about smell for me—cut grass, honeysuckle, must in the old chicken coop, and (when I was very little) a bakery truck that came once a week full of fresh donuts and cakes. In my adolescence, the smells were of Marlboro (mine and my grandmother's), of pot I smoked out behind the old outhouses, and of the rocket fuel coffee my grandmother left percolating all day—coffee that provided a counterbalance to the pot, a poor man's speedball of cannabis and caffeine. And lamb chops—my favorite dish of my grandmother's, something she made for me every visit, the scent emerging from the broiler to blend with coffee and cut grass and a faint whiff of weed.

Contrary to stereotype, however, my grandmother was a horrible—a truly terrible—cook. To be fair, she didn't have much to work with, coming from an Eastern European Jewish background in which *vegetable* meant onion, cabbage, or carrot; the American concept of salad meant iceberg lettuce, beefsteak tomato, and Russian dressing; and meat was kosher, overcooked, and unbearably dry. Add to that the culture of Queens in the 1950s—canned, frozen, pre-packaged food—and my grandmother's meals took on a boiled-to-mush, broiled-to-leather quality. Somehow, though, everyone ate for her, everyone had good appetite at her table, and to her credit she knew where to get the best takeout food, the best delivery, and her refrigerator was always stocked, her cabinets always full of Entenmann's cookies and éclairs—a serious perk for a stoned teenager. She did make a few things well: mushroom-barley soup, and salmon croquettes, and there was something about her tuna salad that people loved. For me, it was always lamb chops and *kasha var-nishkes*—the buckwheat and noodle dish she knew I loved—and marzipan cookies from Adrian's bakery on 73rd Avenue.

But more than anything else, we ate because of her dutiful insistence on feeding—her standard greeting, at the screen door of my grandparents' duplex in Bayside, was never, "Hello," but rather, "Come in, you must be starving." And there was no question of whether or not one would eat, just a question of what and how much. It was understood: everyone ate for Grandma, even when the steak was tough and dry (to the chronic disappointment of my carnivorous uncle, my mother's sister's Sicilian-American husband, who loved his meat blood rare, but ate at my grandmother's behest, like the rest of us).

Dutiful insistence: there's a way in which those words describe my grandmother, in essence. She was loving in her way, and did what was expected of her—she took care of the physical needs of her family, fed everyone, maintained a kind of propriety and structure to things that, if left to my much more casual grandfather, would have degenerated badly. But in her caretaking, in her love, was also a cool distance, a kind of control—in my imagination, a subtle communication that she was a bit better than all this. She had been an excellent student, a "bright girl," and came (according to my mother) from a lineage of rabbis. Her mother, Hinda, had been a flamboyant character—prone to dancing and wearing wild scarves, with a basement full of herbs and vials of medicine, with chants and spells and charms to avert the evil eye. My grandmother's cool propriety, her adherence to duty, was perhaps a reaction to her mother's colorful, iconoclastic nature, but at the same time was a comment on her own restrained power, her inability in that world, at that time, in that culture, to be anything other than a dutiful wife and mother.

In the mid-1990s, a few years before my grandmother passed away, there was a monumental blizzard, and business and services all over New York were shutting down—it was on the news, even in the Bay Area. Now alone, my grandmother still lived in the duplex in Bayside in which she'd raised her children and she and my grandfather had shared their life. I called her to see how she was (I'm not sure what I could have done if she wasn't OK, but in my own dutiful way I had to call); my grandmother answered in a panic: "It's horrible, it's terrible."

"What, grandma, what's happening?"

"It's terrible, it's terrible."

"Grandma, are you OK?"

"It's horrible, you wouldn't believe..."

"Grandma, what's wrong?"

"They canceled my beauty parlor appointment."

Aside from blizzard-based beauty parlor closures, she never complained, my grandmother, and I have no way of knowing if my thoughts on her inner life have any bearing on reality. She did, on occasion, when my grandfather came home from work and planted himself in the chair in front of the TV, as she served dinner and cleaned up the mess—never sitting at the table herself, always hovering—comment, "So, when do I get to relax?" But it's not as if her love wasn't genuine, as if she didn't care for her family; it was simply as if, embedded in all of her love and duty and, of course, feeding, there was a wish for her own life, for a life more consistent with her nature and with her self-perception than the one she had.

TRAUMA AND EXILE

"There's a moon in my body, but I can't see it! A moon and a sun. A drum never touched by hands, beating, and I can't hear it!"
——KABIR

In my late twenties and early thirties, I became intensely involved in the study and practice of Kabbalah and other Jewish mystical traditions. I was finishing graduate school in psychology at the time, and the walls of my room were completely lined with full bookshelves—texts on mysticism, religion, psychology, and philosophy. My ulcerative colitis was in chronic flare-up during this period, and I was in a deep depression as well, in part because of my physical illness. I desperately sought relief in the spiritual practices in which I was engaged—in the community, in the ritual, and in the textual study—but despite this I felt more and more overwhelmed, bleak, distant from myself, from hope, from any sense of connection with the divine. One day, sitting in the middle of the floor in my study, surrounded by bookshelf upon bookshelf, I collapsed in tears and had the (perhaps obvious) realization that for me, god is not to be found in books—to be sure, a very un-Jewish thing to realize.

Everything began to shift after this, and I moved in other directions that were more useful, more authentic for me. But this period of exile—in the form of bleakness, devastation, and disconnection—was necessary, I think, in order for me to emerge into a different form of connection, both with myself and in my relationship to the divine.

In Judaism, the term *galut* describes the exile, the wanderings of the Jews—first, our desert wanderings after the exodus from Egypt; later, our Babylonian exile; and ultimately, our diaspora in general. In a less historical, more spiritual context, *galut* is often used to describe the relationship between the individual and the divine—the interplay of imminence and transcendence, the experience of periods of connection to and disconnection from the Source—much in the same vein as the experience of longing and distance described by the great Sufi poets. In this sense the term is a wonderful parallel to the way in which mainstream recovery describes the need for (and development of) a relationship with a higher power—the process of desperation, surrender, and connection.

But in a more internal sense, the term *galut*, for me, evokes the experience of trauma—the disconnection from embodiment, directionality, subjectivity of which I've already written. Exile is an apt description of the direct experience of trauma, and in that description lies a thread of the possibility of recovery. That evocation of inner wandering—written of more substantively by Jungian analyst Dr. Steven Joseph—evokes Jung's description of the circumambulation of the psyche, the meandering process of following of one's red thread so necessary for movement toward wholeness.

To take the metaphor further, for me the language of exile, *galut*, is deeply linked to the phenomenon of intergenerational trauma. In a very literal sense, this term describes the experience of being severed from family, from ancestral lineage, from cultural background; it describes the experience of being in exile from the matrix of heritage as a result of centuries of traumatization, oppression, and disruption of culture and cultural identity. Such is the experience of historically oppressed and traumatized cultural groups, whether Jews or Irish or Native Americans or many others, and also the experience, I believe, of the descendants of those who have been the oppressors—for in my experience as a clinician, traumatization and oppression affect the psyches of all involved, not simply those who are on the receiving end.

Deeper still, there's a way in which *galut* describes a kind of inner exile that's transmitted intergenerationally—an experience of darkness, of silence, of disconnection, of not knowing why the feelings of distance, deprivation, and longing for connection are so pervasive. But in this is more than simply a metaphorical—or even mythological—description of psychological experience. For me, it's been essential to connect with a cultural, tribal metaphor that not only re-frames my experience in new language, that not only gives it meaning and significance, but that invokes my own indigenous cultural symbol— that re-establishes connection to the ancestral realm, calling on my ancestors through that connection, and engaging a process of transforming their experience as it is lived in me.

This is a different kind of metaphor of healing, a true living symbol that accesses processes of healing that exist outside of immediate awareness, that works in subtle and mysterious ways. In my experience, both personally and clinically, to transform personal and ancestral traumatization, to return from exile in both cultural framework and embodied, energetic connection to subjectivity, it is essential to reconnect with these indigenous processes of healing that already exist deep in the psyche. In this process, nothing new need be created; it is only necessary to find ways to connect with what is already present, and if there is any gift in the experience of intergenerational injury, it is the impetus toward this symbolic, mythic, ancestral reconnection.

HUNGRY GHOSTS

"What we call rational grounds for our beliefs are often extremely irrational attempts to justify our instincts."
—THOMAS HENRY HUXLEY

I'm often aware of the presence of ghosts—of lingering energies that remain unresolved, unacknowledged, adrift; of the ghosts of my own past, of course, but also of those from the ancestral realm. In one sense this ghostliness is simply a psychological experience, a feeling of something lingering, hungry, unredeemed, but there is also a literal way in which this is *fact*: an embodied connection to another world, to other parts of myself, to those who came before, from whom I have inherited this body, this life.

Dr. Gabor Mate writes of addiction as the realm of hungry ghosts, and this is in many ways certainly the case—he evokes the classical Buddhist image, a starving being, a ghost with a neck so long and narrow it cannot derive nourishment from anything it takes in, but so full of desire, longing, that it can only wander, seeking. Like most addicts, I know all too well that ghostly state of being, that hunger, that unquenchable desire.

After my graduation from Phoenix House, I worked for a time as a prevention counselor in their drug education program. I wore a suit, and with my colleagues was sent out to New York area schools to present a prevention curriculum: workshop after workshop on decision-making skills, and on the process of addiction. I was happy to be working for my alma mater, but in truth wanted to work more clinically with addicts seeking recovery, so I applied for a job at another residential treatment program, and was interviewed by the clinical director and program director—both Jews, both recovering heroin addicts. They knew my background, both addiction and culture, and they had one significant question for me: in my addiction, had I been a dabbler, someone who had gotten out of control on party drugs and gotten into trouble? Or was I a *chazer*—the Yiddish term for pig, glutton, greedy bastard: a die-hard junkie who couldn't get enough, no matter what. To them, it was important that this background, this familiarity with that kind of deep hunger be part of my history. To be a clinician, from their perspective, one had to know the inner world of that hungry ghost.

I was a *chazer*. I got the job.

But there's more to this phenomenon than the desire, hunger, intense addiction that can so easily be attributed to early childhood wounding, to insufficient empathy or misplaced love during periods of developmental vulnerability. And there's more to this phenomenon than the unavoidable residue of living in a culture that instills desire, that feeds off the constant longing for whatever is just out of reach, and that fosters a fantasy of satisfaction through consumerist grasping. Of course, these developmental and societal underpinnings of ghostly hunger are legitimate, deserving of acknowledgment and attention, but there is more.

In some Daoist traditions, it's understood that this longing, this hunger—whether for love, money, drugs, food, and so on—comes not from the desperation induced by cultural and economic dynamics, nor from childhood injuries, but from the inherited, embodied experiences of one's unsettled ancestors: ghosts. It arises from unresolved experience, from the death throes of someone murdered, or dead of starvation, or bloody on a battlefield, or dying while thinking of a lover they've left behind. The permutations are endless, but the experience is universal: the sense of being stuck or out of place, the sense of longing, the presence of the chronic thought, *I could have, I should have, if only I could…*

If only. This is the common denominator of that ghostly energy, however it is derived, however it is defined, however it is symbolized. To understand this, it is not necessary that one believe in a literal ancestral being, in a historical connection to the unresolved life of a specific individual—although in my experience this is indeed true—but rather it is necessary that there be an openness to transforming this ghostliness through something other than constantly seeking to feed its hungry, never-satisfied mouth.

For me, this ancestral understanding of ghostly energy is important in that it gives it an embodied root—it takes this experience out of the free-floating quality so endemic to ghostliness, and within the framework of Chinese medicine, it grounds this phenomenon in something both physiological and energetic: in the kidney, in the *jing*, in the physical connection with our prenatal energy, with all who came before. It sets up the possibility of not just psychological and behavioral (and even spiritual) intervention, but of energetic and somatic transformation as well. It provides a literal, embodied reality for the psychological experience of intergenerational transmission of trauma, and it offers a possibility for resolution—and perhaps more importantly, an opportunity for reconnection.

RICK

"I'm an old-time smugglin' man,
I know just what to do.
I sell guns to the Arabs,
I sell dynamite to the Jews."
—TIM HARDIN

I first met Rick soon after he and my mother started seeing each other. My mother had come from Hawaii to Connecticut for my high school graduation, and was staying with her cousin in Westport; she was still living with Steve at the time, but the night before graduation she and her cousin went out drinking, and my mom met the sociopathically charming Rick, quickly broke off her relationship with Steve, and, I think, never looked back.

Like many others, I idealized Rick. Quintessentially charismatic, he was an attorney who, in an earlier stage in his life, served a couple of years in the federal penitentiary in Danbury for drug smuggling. At the time I knew him, he was highly paid for defending drug dealers; he drank vast quantities of Wild Turkey, and pontificated on just about everything, but especially on the importance of keeping one's word—often with Tim Hardin, one of his favorites, playing "Don't Make Promises You Can't Keep" in the background. I never knew the full story of Rick's arrest and imprisonment, but always had the sense that there was a betrayal involved, that Rick's lingering bitterness derived less from the time served than from the loyalties that had been ruptured. To him, loyalty was everything.

Rick grew up in Bridgeport, a tough Irish kid with a firefighter father. He came up in the '60s, amidst drugs and revolution; his revolutionary spirit, though not entirely broken by his time in prison, had become somehow distorted, turned in upon itself. His once-upon-a-time commitment to political upheaval, to transformation, was now booze-fueled braggadocio; though well-intentioned in many ways, his desire to become an attorney so as to make sure others didn't suffer his fate was now a kind of narcissistic revelry in his own gift of gab, and in the adulation of the veritable sea of degenerates—myself included—with whom he surrounded himself.

For some reason, Rick loved the fact that I was a prep school kid; he introduced me as his friend from Choate, let me run up his bar tabs, introduced me to bikers and deadheads and pimps and dealers of all stripes, people of the sort I had always wanted to meet—or more accurately, people I had always wanted to be. And I did, indeed, become one of them—to the point that during that period I once even sold a quantity of really bad cocaine to my mom. It was from an ounce I'd gotten on credit; I'd promptly freebased the majority of it, then realized

I needed to sell enough to pay my source, so cut the remainder so heavily it was next to useless. I remember feeling horribly guilty, but it was never clear to me whether I felt bad for selling cocaine to my mother, or for selling her such stepped-on rubbish at full retail price.

As the wheels began to come off their life together, my mom and Rick, encumbered with debt and fleeing from burned bridges, began to make geographic moves in the vain hope that something would be different somewhere else: the Big Island, Martha's Vineyard, Ireland (where Rick claimed Irish citizenship and immediately went on the dole), and eventually back to Kauai. In the process of mutual alcoholic self-destruction, they ran through every remaining cent, every resource, every friendship and relationship either of them had.

In these locales, drunken fights between my mother and Rick became more frequent, and the drama intensified. I would get phone calls from my mother, slurred and crying, begging me to come pick her up because Rick had again hit her, egging me on to punch him out, even to kill him. I remember showing up at their place (in Puako, or Connecticut, or whichever other place it might have been that time around) ready to get into a brawl, ready to defend my mother's honor—only to find her bruised and angry, to learn that they'd gotten drunk together on tequila, that she'd attacked him with a pitchfork, and that

he'd punched her rather than being run through with
its tines. Time after time, in the face of these scenar-
ios, I got in my car and drove away, sometimes taking
my mother with me and dropping her someplace safe,
sometimes leaving on my own and leaving her to the
remnants of her life and the consequences of her own
insanity—myself not yet in recovery, but quite done
with their drama nonetheless.

To her credit, my mother eventually stopped
drinking, and made a number of changes in her
life, including severing her ties with Rick. Tired of
being hit, I think perhaps she was even more tired
of who she had become with Rick—tired of her own
anger, and of the destructiveness that was given a
toxic voice through that relationship. Rick, though,
remained simply himself, and a few years later I
heard through the grapevine that he had died of a
metastasized melanoma—the result of a combination of his fair Irish skin, the Hawaiian sun, and a
botched surgery: an ignominious end to a colorful,
painful life.

More than anything else, around Rick I remember feeling a combination of dread and excitement—
a sense of intrigue and danger that was both entic-
ing and horrible, that required massive amounts of
alcohol and cocaine in order for anyone to keep up.
We had a genuine liking for each other, Rick and
I—or, at least, I liked him as much as one can like
someone involved with one's mother in such a brutal

relationship. I hated Rick for what he had done, both to himself and to my mother, probably in some sense in the way in which he hated himself. But I loved him, too—in a way in which, in the face of his drunken smirk, his stories and his passion, it was impossible not to. Rick told me often that if I ever got arrested to say absolutely nothing other than that I was represented by counsel, and to call him immediately, and I knew that in spite of everything, regardless of his state of inebriation, regardless of the state of his relationship with my mother, that he would keep his promise—that he would show up.

Shame and
the Language of Disease

*"The moral flabbiness born of the exclusive
worship of the bitch-goddess success. That—
with the squalid cash interpretation put on
the word 'success'—is our national disease."*
— WILLIAM JAMES

*"The hardest choice in life is to see things as
they truly are, and to call them by their right
names."*
— BENJAMIN R. TONG

Psychoanalysts use the term *overdetermined* to
describe the reality that events, experiences, and
symbols can have more than one legitimate meaning.
As in Akira Kurosawa's powerful film *Rashomon*,
multiple truths are possible—stories from different
angles that bear the reality of experience, that do
not exclude the possibility that other stories are also
true, even if some of them are inconsistent with each
other. For me, the concept of addiction as a *disease*
is like this—it elicits multiple possibilities, various
interpretations based on perspective, context, and,
importantly, history.

Historically, labeling addiction as a disease was
a well-intentioned (and, I think, generally positive)

attempt to shift from the prevailing ideology of addiction as a moral failing toward a more compassionate perception of addiction as a medical disorder—essentially, moving from hopeless flaw to treatable condition. Often framed as a spiritual malady having to do with a kind of disconnection from a higher power, the term *disease* is also used to describe addiction as a chronic biomedical condition, complete with genetic predisposition, and requiring lifelong maintenance. (As an aside, I prefer the term *hereditary* to the term *genetic* because it allows for the possibility of different forms of inheritance—for example, ancestral transmission—that go beyond biological mechanism. As the burgeoning field of epigenetics would suggest, inherited aspects of addiction are indeed a reality, but in my personal and professional experience this phenomenon of heredity is not solely biomedical, but also energetic, transpersonal.)

I tend to think of the root of my addiction as a chronic, pervasive, sometimes uncontrollable desire to be elsewhere. Of course this is a bit of an oversimplification, and there are certainly both precursors and sequelae to this phenomenon, manifestations in work, relationships, self-perception, and elsewhere. But fundamentally this process is about the drive to be other than where I am, and other than who I am—and in this sense, for me, this basic urge to check out is also rooted in the experience of shame. From this perspective, while the concept of addiction as disease is useful on many levels, for me it has a strong tendency to reinforce the shame-based perception that I am somehow essentially damaged.

There's a historical context to this, a context which is quite significant in my struggle with the language of disease. That is, mainstream approaches to recovery—from which the language of disease emerges—are derived from Christianity (specifically, from the Oxford Group), in which the concept of original sin is subtly vestigial. However, the concept of original sin is part of neither my cultural framework nor my religious background, so at best it is, in my inner world, irrelevant. More importantly, the residue of centuries of oppression and traumatization of the Jews of Europe (and elsewhere) is alive and well in my personal, cultural, even somatic experience of shame. For me, however well-intentioned, the language of disease triggers a kind of historical re-enactment of oppression, a traumatically-rooted sense of inherent flaw—and this only deepens my shame-based, addictive urge to be someone, or somewhere, else.

To be clear, I am neither criticizing Christianity nor any approach to recovery, but rather am attempting to understand the language that has such impact on me by naming the context in which it arises— and to describe the ways in which I personally find the language of disease to be a trigger for this legacy of shame. Neither am I saying that this language is inherently problematic—I certainly acknowledge the utility of that language in providing, among other things, freedom from culturally entrenched moralism. And I am not in any form denigrating the necessity for lifelong maintenance of recovery—although I prefer the term *practice* over the term *maintenance*. In any case, this is not a universal critique, but rather an elaboration on my own struggle in which the historical underpinnings of language are just as important as the historical realities of my heritage, my family, myself.

The personal experience of this process is such that when I hear myself described in the language of disease, I do not feel the relief that I know is present for others—the freedom from moralistic judgment, or the clarity that might result from an explanation for one's addiction. Rather, I feel shame, distance from myself, and a lack of connection with body, with my own energy, with anything I consider to be divine. From here, I can very easily fall further into a shame-based sense that there is something wrong with me because I don't relate to this language in that way that others seem to—and that, somehow, I should. But rather than continue that downward spiral, it is vital that I choose to remain connected with what is real, relevant, true for me—and for me, an overdetermined perspective on the language of disease and on my experience of the historical legacy of shame is essential in the recovery of an authentic relationship with my own energy, with my own perceptions, with a trusting heart.

TRAUMA, QIGONG, AND TRUST

"The man who strikes is not a man at all. The striking sword is not a sword. And for myself, the person who is about to cut, in a flash of lightning, it will be like cutting through the breeze that blows across the spring sky. It is the mind that absolutely does not stop."
                                    —TAKUAN SOHO

Trauma is, among other things, an embodied experience, and a variety of approaches to the bodily aspects of trauma can be of significant value in resolving post-traumatic residue—notably, among others, Peter Levine's process of Somatic Experiencing™. Many somatic approaches go quite deep, delving into mindful awareness of embodied experience, the physiology of trauma and nervous system arousal, and even the archetypal layers of the psyche that are accessible through embodiment. Both personally and professionally, I've found a variety of forms of bodywork, embodied trauma work, and somatic psychotherapy to be powerfully transformative, but in my experience, the core phenomenon underlying the somatic, physiological, and psychological sequelae of trauma is a disruption of energy: trauma is, in the most fundamental sense, an energetic disorder.

In the haunting film *Donnie Darko*, there's a scene in which rippling, tubular fields emerge from people's chests; these long, energetic phenomena seem to both meander and lead, and there's a kind of directionality implied, a connectedness to forward movement, to intention, perhaps even to a fated path. In a symbolic sense, this is a significant image for the experience of trauma—for me, it is exactly this energetic experience of directionality that is injured, stunted, sometimes even severed by the experience of both personal and transpersonal trauma.

In this context, much as I value recent developments in embodied trauma work, it's the energetic practices emerging from the Daoist tradition that have been most helpful for me in trauma recovery. There's something extraordinarily powerful in the long history of these practices, and in the directness of their approach in working with energy. Also, the lineage of these practices seems to resonate deeply in an intergenerational sense; something about this legacy resonates with the deepest aspects of my own inherited legacy of trauma. In any case, these practices have had tremendous value for me not just in physical health, but also in the recovery of a relationship to energy—in the process of recovery of a kind of energetic integrity.

At core, what I'm referring to is *qi*—of which there are many forms and many understandings, and of which a thorough discussion is far beyond the scope of this work—and *qigong*, a plethora of traditional practices that develop, focus, even heal one's energy. Within the broad framework of *qigong*, some practices cultivate *qi*, others emphasize sensitivity and awareness of it, and still others—both medical and martial—focus on its purposeful application. Mindfulness, awareness, and somatic connection are important components of all of these, but beyond simple awareness and embodiment, *qigong* is a real energetic phenomenon; it is about *qi*, which in an embodied sense can be injured, drained, blocked, or otherwise put in disarray by a variety of climatic and psychological causes—including trauma, both directly experienced and inherited.

Chinese medicine (which in essence is itself a form of *qigong*) is profoundly helpful in understanding the dynamics, the diagnostics of injuries to *qi* in both organ systems and meridians, from both external causes and traumatic events. But Chinese medicine intervention (acupuncture, herbs, and so on) aside, in terms of direct connection and energetic integrity, what's been most helpful for me is the formal practice of *qigong*—and in particular, the practice of what are often referred to as internal martial arts, of which *taijiquan* is the best known. While these martial *qigong* practices are essentially fighting arts, they are not solely for combat, but also develop both *qi* itself, and one's relationship with and sensitivity to it. (*Xingyiquan*, the martial embodiment of the bear, which is much more linear than *taiji* and its other cousins, has been particularly helpful for me in developing connection with my own forward momentum, my own directionality.)

My teachers, Drs. Benjamin Tong and Randy Sugawara, both have backgrounds in clinical psychology as well as extensive internal martial arts training, and have been working with exactly this kind of phenomenon for many years. In fact, Dr. Sugawara works specifically with addiction and relapse (as well as anxiety, depression, and related issues) through *qigong* practice as development of relationship with *qi*. Fundamentally, though, whether martial or not, and whether or not they are psychological in intent, these traditional practices are indeed about developing energy, but beyond that are also about developing a kind of relationship with one's deeper processes in a very literal, energetic sense. From my perspective, this develops in a form that is very different from other forms of somatic trauma work, in a way that establishes an actual connection with the source of one's being—in a way that is directly applicable to the experience of energy having been severed, stuck, stunted, or in some other way altered by trauma.

Putting aside for the moment any methodology of recovery from trauma—whether through *qigong* or other psychological or somatic processes—I think this energetic understanding of trauma is critically important for the mutual processes of recovery from trauma and recovery from addiction: these two processes, so often intimately linked, are in some ways diametrically opposed. Ultimately, an energetic perspective on trauma suggests a need to develop the capacity to trust one's own perceptions and sensibilities, to follow one's energy—to be aware of what feels like flow and what feels like stoppage, of what feels like abundance and what feels like restriction. But in my experience, much of mainstream recovery, rooted in the concept of disease, reinforces an essential distrust of one's perceptions, of one's decision-making processes. So, while I certainly recognize the importance of consulting others in decision-making (especially in early recovery), at a certain point this only reinforces the ideology that one's most vital processes and perceptions are fundamentally suspect. This reinforcement of distrust in some sense undermines the process necessary for recovery from personal and intergenerational trauma, and this, in my experience, is a significant dynamic for those who—like me—have both addiction and trauma history and who at points become stuck in their recovery from both. Unfortunately, I don't have a clear solution for this conundrum, but in fact I'm not sure it needs a solution—I'm not sure it's necessary that all paths and approaches are consistent, or even compatible with each other. What is necessary, for me anyway, is the act of naming this conflict, for in some sense this simple acknowledgment of contradiction is in and of itself an act of connection with a fundamental aspect of energetic integrity.

SADIE AND DELLA

"'What do these children do without story-books?' Naftali asked.

And Reb Zebulun replied: "They have to make do. Storybooks aren't bread. You can live without them.'

'I couldn't live without them.' Naftali said."
—ISAAC BASHEVIS SINGER

Sadie and Della lived in a duplex on Avenue O in Brooklyn. My grandfather's older sisters, they had lived alone since their husbands had passed away, puttering around their oversize house, speaking as if with one mind. Uncle Stan was Della's late husband, and had been the kindest of men, everyone's favorite; he sold pennants at Shea Stadium and, when I was a child, gifted me with a plethora of Mets and Jets pennants—the old felt ones that felt so good to the touch, and which I taped to the wall over my bed. Uncle Stan was a fan of Jell-O with milk poured over the top, a strange delicacy that was always served on those rare occasions when my parents and I visited, and which I loved. Uncle Harry, Sadie's late husband, was a different sort; kind as well, he was more distant, and smelled of cigars—a smell I loved as a child—and always wore a yarmulke. Even when I was little, he shook my hand like a grownup, which was both painful and a little thrilling.

By the 1980s, Sadie had long since raised her children; her son Ben, a tax attorney, had moved to Westchester and raised children of his own. Della had never had children; she lived in the top half of the duplex, Sadie in the lower half, but more often than not when I visited with my grandparents they were both at Sadie's place, having the same conversation they always had, sitting on the doily-covered couch in Sadie's living room. There was always a bowl with broken-up Hershey bars or kisses on the coffee table—which, stoned as I was, was the highlight of the visit for me—and a bowl of sourballs or some other hard candy. Della would unwrap a sourball, and pop it in her mouth:

Della: "I have a sour taste in my mouth."

Sadie: "What sour taste? If you wouldn't eat so many sourballs you wouldn't have a sour taste."

Della: "No, I need the sourball, I have a sour taste."

And so on, ad infinitum.

Visits to Sadie and Della were a regular occurrence on those occasions when I had a pass from boarding school and would stay with my grandparents in Bayside for a weekend. Saturday afternoon meant the ritual journey to Brooklyn: my grandfather would put some tools in the trunk of his Buick Regal to fix whatever plumbing or electrical problem Sadie had developed during the past week. I'd find a way, surreptitiously, to get high, and we'd pile into the car. On arrival, my grandfather would get to work with his handyman duties; I'd help him, or, preferably, raid the Hershey bowl and answer everyone's repetitive questions about school, about my mother, about when my parents were getting back together.

Dinner was always sparse—Kraft macaroni and cheese, gefilte fish with horseradish, iceberg lettuce, and a loaf of rye bread with butter, the same menu every time. One box of mac and cheese for the five of us, which, even with plentiful bread, always meant my grandfather and I would need a late evening turkey sandwich when we got back to Bayside. He loved the gefilte fish, though, and especially the gelatin from the jar, which he was always served; I could barely tolerate gefilte fish, let alone the gelatin, but in the absence of anything else to eat would slather it with the horseradish and choke it down. My grandmother, when we left, would comment on Sadie's miserliness—the miniscule dinner, her refusal to spend money to have an actual handyman come fix things, her unwillingness to buy a new refrigerator which she needed badly. Sadie had the money, but came from an era in which expenditures were limited to essentials; it was just that her perception of what was essential was, perhaps, a bit distorted.

After dinner we'd play poker, the five of us, but in a routine sort of way. Everyone knew what the expected bet was for whatever hand they had—a nickel for a pair, a dime for two pair or three of a kind, a quarter for a better hand than that. It wasn't poker, really, but rather yet another weekly ritual; I would bet randomly, or bluff, just to confuse them, just because. I would shuffle faro style, which they loved: "Look how he *teschles* the cards," they'd say, Sadie or Della, it didn't matter which one, the two of them having lived together so long they were two halves of the same person—Della, sweet and introverted, Sadie the dominant one, smart and outspoken.

The last time I remember visiting them, when my grandparents and I arrived, something was different. In front of the duplex had been a small patch of lawn alongside the walkway—very small, really, perhaps eight feet by eight feet. The lawn had always before been well-trimmed—Sadie and Della paid one of the neighborhood *goyim* to cut it on a biweekly basis. I guess they had finally gotten tired of spending money on something they, in their uniquely predictable way, considered a non-essential; this time when we arrived, the lawn had been ripped out and replaced with concrete, but concrete that had been painted green.

To their unified mind, what was the difference?

Mindfulness and
the Hell of Knowing

"Better to reign in Hell,
than to serve in Heaven"
　　　　　—John Milton

"Only don't know."
　　　　　　　—Seung Sahn

In the context of trauma, the severing of a connection to one's vitality is a form of survival. For me, this was certainly the case—I disconnected from myself out of the urge for self preservation; not to have done so would have left that vital part of me vulnerable to attack. Disconnecting was protective; it was necessary in order to maintain the illusion that what was going on around me was not as chaotic as it really was. I needed to create the fiction that somehow, if I found the right means, I could manage this unmanageability—a fiction so contrary to reality that my most basic sensibilities needed to be submerged so that they wouldn't come into conflict with the fantasy that I had control over something, anything.

This disconnection emerged as a spiral of mental planning, strategizing, and obsessive thinking about what was happening, what might happen, what it all meant. Quite simply, I needed things to make sense in order to feel safe, and they didn't, so I lived in the fragmentation of my most fundamental perceptions, in a severing of connection to embodiment. In the absence of a relationship to my energetic root, I found myself relying on cognition, caught in a desperate need to know what was really unknowable. I lay awake hours into the night, immersed in the stories and structures of my mind; I withdrew from the world, often through vehicles such as books and television—vehicles that allowed me to become even further lost in the protective loops of pseudo-knowing.

The five phases (five elements) theory of Chinese medicine offers a valuable energetic-psychological interpretation of this dynamic. Whereas the fire element (heart) is referred to as the "emperor," the wood element (liver) is referred to as the "general," largely serving the functions of planning and strategizing. Water (kidney, the source of prenatal *qi*, the connection to ancestral vitality) nourishes wood, but is disrupted by fear, by the shock of trauma; in the experience of trauma, wood becomes disconnected from its water root, floating out of control. Wood keeps earth (spleen, cognition) in control, but when wood is disconnected from its source of nourishment (water), excessive reliance on planning and strategizing ensues. This over-activity of wood then over-controls earth, impeding and even damaging it. Consequently, cognition too becomes impeded, looping into rumination, becoming obsessive as a result of the traumatic disconnection of water and wood.

Changing this dynamic is easier said than done. Letting go of knowing—developing faith—is an essential and extremely valuable process within mainstream recovery, but as with the above example from Chinese medicine, there is also an energetic, embodied solution, a possible resolution to an excessive reliance on cognition that disrupts intuitive knowing. Both Chinese medicine and depth psychotherapy legitimize such non-linear forms of knowing; the great existential psychologist Rollo May said psychotherapists should leave theory at the door of the consulting room—welcoming the unknown, cultivating a stance of not knowing as a means to transformation. But while Chinese medicine, psychotherapy, and mainstream recovery all in their own way cultivate not knowing, for me the simplest, most direct, most clear means by which to enter this realm is through the practice of mindfulness meditation.

Not knowing is terrifying, especially for someone such as myself, so reliant on knowing as a means of self-protection, as a way to evade the vulnerability of uncertainty. But by not knowing, it becomes possible to feel my way into that old place of disconnection, to experience the reality of it, and to begin anew through a direct, non-cognitive encounter with this severed aspect of myself. Mindfulness practice allows this, creates this possibility (and, of course, much more); beyond this, mindfulness meditation is an act of profound trust in the present moment. For those of us with traumatic history, trust (whether in ourselves or in the world) is in and of itself extraordinarily difficult, largely because the disruption of trust is at the very foundation of the injury. But in order to allow reconnection to form, it is necessary to leap into the unknown, into not knowing, no matter how terrifying—and in so doing, to confront the fear that lies at the root of the rupture. In this process, the freeing act of trust entailed in simple mindfulness is both deeply healing and profoundly humbling.

Toxic Loyalty and
Ancestral Transformation

"Frank Lopez: You know what a chazer is?
Tony Montana: No, Frank, you tell me. What
is a chazer?
Frank Lopez: It's a Yiddish word for 'pig.' See,
the guy, he wants more than what he needs.
He don't fly straight no more."

—*Scarface*

In the context in which I grew up—amidst pot growers, drug dealers, bikers, criminals, drunks, and degenerates of all sorts—the emphasis on loyalty was pervasive. Sometimes overt, sometimes subtle, I always knew that there was an expectation of, as they say in the movies, being a stand-up guy. This meant a lot of things: it meant you didn't cheat your friends (not even a little), and you didn't hit on their girlfriends; it meant you didn't say anything if you got busted—you didn't roll over on anyone, ever; it meant there were people you could scam, and people you just didn't, and you knew instinctively who they were; and it meant you knew who truly had your back, who was loyal to you.

I had two "business" partners whom I trusted implicitly. When the three of us first met, there was an immediate and spontaneous sense of connection that ran deep. Like Liu Bei, Guan Yu, and Zhang Fei in the peach garden in the classic Chinese epic Romance of the Three Kingdoms, we were instant brothers. Through all of our debauchery and illicit activity, none of us ever stole from each other—not even to the extent of holding out when it came to paying our share of meals or gas. And I know, to this day, that regardless of how infrequent our contact might be, I can trust those compatriots—that any of us would still show up for the others if there were a need. (Of those two, one never became addicted to heroin, and eventually straightened out his life. The other, my closest junkie running buddy, entered recovery at the same time I did. We still share the same clean date, and no matter what, we call each other every year on our mutual anniversary.)

At one point the three of us were moving into an apartment together, but needed a fourth house-mate to fill an additional room. We invited a mutual friend to live with us—and since he was living with us, we included him in our dealing activities. We soon started to receive complaints from our customers about short counts, and it became clear that he was taking a small amount from each bag of pot or bindle of coke he sold, perhaps to sell surreptitiously, perhaps simply for his own use. This was unforgiveable, not just because of his dishonesty with us, his partners, nor because of the damage to our reputations, but because if he'd needed drugs or money, if he'd come to the rest of us, we would have shared whatever we had. To steal what would have been freely given was, perhaps, a worse betrayal than the theft itself. (Ultimately, I confronted him, and he and I got into a physical altercation, soon after which he moved out and was entirely ostracized.)

But there are, of course, both positive and negative implications to loyalty. Although in one sense it is the very fabric of human connection, there are also ways in which entrenched loyalties can become a catalyst for self-destruction, both in active addiction and in recovery. At the root of this phenomenon is loyalty to family, to the inherited matrix of beliefs about life and about self—a web of allegiances that, though perhaps destructive, fraught with denial and self-sabotage, are forged in the desire for love and connection. In a toxic environment, the drive for natural, positive human needs to be met becomes twisted; it turns into a willingness to destroy oneself in order to maintain the fantasy that these allegiances will bring the desired nourishment that is somehow eternally just out of reach. Over the years, in clinical settings, it's been my experience that a vast number of people leave or otherwise sabotage their treatment because of implicitly or overtly manipulated loyalties to family—to their deeply entrenched need to remain in these familiar roles, however destructive they might be.

Developing an awareness of my own willingness to sacrifice myself for loyalty—and learning to combat this tendency—has been central in my recovery. Early on, when I left the Lower East Side to enter treatment at Phoenix House, I was reviled by several of my addict friends for abandoning them—as if I should have remained with them in self-destruction rather than getting help. I felt guilt and fear at the prospect of moving forward, of leaving the web of mutual self-destruction we had created, yet I knew that my departure was a necessary choice between life and death. And when, after completing treatment and working for Phoenix House for a year or so, I decided to depart for a new job at another treatment program, I was accused of disloyalty to those who had saved my life. It was as if I were expected to give up one problematic loyalty for another, when the essential need was the development of my own integrity, the cultivation of loyalty to a relationship with my own deepest being. I had at least begun to understand that, despite my concern for my former friends, despite my deep gratitude to Phoenix House, my sense of loyalty would kill me—by sucking me back into active addiction, or, perhaps even worse, by leading me into an inauthentic life, so disconnected from my own integrity that it would become a kind of living death.

Like most addicts, I know all too well the realm of living death—the half-life embodied in active addiction, in the ghostly existence of seeking and using and seeking some more, in desperation, in constant deprivation, in fear. Even in recovery, at times this feeling of disconnection arises, this sense that I'm not living in my integrity—that (often out of allegiance to a deep and complex web of loyalties) I am somehow living a life not entirely my own. For me, there is a connection between the living death of disconnection and the struggle with an underlying set of loyalties—loyalties embedded in the deepest reaches of my embodied, energetic being, loyalties bequeathed through my family, entwined in my DNA, rooted in my essence. These allegiances are, in my inner world, the residue of intergenerational trauma, of successive generations of fear—an ancestral foundation to a loyalty-based matrix of self-destruction. In my energetic relationship with this phenomenon I have too many times remained static, even moved backwards or become self-destructive, so as not to challenge the sense of panic that arises out of the possibility of success, of fulfillment, of life itself—the sense that somehow by moving forward I would be abandoning *them*. In trauma, in chaos, hope itself means vulnerability, even danger, and in some sense to move forward from this place of fear is a kind of disloyalty—one I know all too well. And I know that this toxic loyalty to my ancestors' trauma is a truly demonic process that flourishes in the leavings of my own self-destruction.

I know, too, that challenging this destructive energy, remaining loyal to the deepest relationship with myself, is a necessity for my recovery, and it is also a kind of loving loyalty to my ancestors—a different form of loyalty that allows them freedom, perhaps even rest. In my struggle with toxic loyalty and this dynamic of self-destruction, it is not that they want me to accede, to fall backward into the depths of martyrdom, but rather that they want of me what they cannot do for themselves—they want me to live, physically, energetically, spiritually, fully. Through my engagement with these archaic loyalties, through my emergence from them, through allowing myself to have a life beyond that ghostly realm, they too can become whole and thus can leave behind their fear and trauma. What they need of me is to surpass them, not in the form of possessions or achievements or other aspects of worldly life, but rather in the capacity to live authentically, in my own integrity—to live with loyalty, but loyalty redefined.

WITHOUT LIMITS

"Never get out of the boat. Absolutely god-damn right. Unless you were goin' all the way."
—CAPTAIN WILLARD, *Apocalypse Now*

"Avoid all needle drugs. The only dope worth shooting is Richard Nixon."
—ABBIE HOFFMAN

When it came to drugs, my mother's only rule was: don't take acid and don't do heroin. Well intentioned, her dictum was based on having seen friends go off the deep end with those particular substances. But, of course, the one thing I was told not to do elicited a fascination with the forbidden, a desire to push the envelope—to find a limit of some kind. In a world in which almost nothing was out of bounds, in which just about anything was acceptable, acid and heroin were, of course, all I wanted.

I was ten, I think, or perhaps eleven, when my mother first caught me with pot. She didn't actually catch me with it; rather, she found a couple of bits of leaf on the floor of my room, remnants of a joint I'd rolled earlier that day. When I came home she confronted me, and I told her I'd been smoking on and off for a couple of years, ever since my friend Gavin and I had stolen and smoked a roach from his mom's cigarette pack when we were in the third grade. It was the Big Island in the 1970s, and pot was ubiquitous—growers were everywhere, driving brand-new pickup trucks they'd paid for in cash. Many of them, as I recall, had recently been discharged from the military after tours in Vietnam, and were somehow reenacting jungle warfare with booby traps and small arms in the local rain forest. My friends and I always knew, when hiking, never to go off the trail.

In this culture and era, when my mom found pot in my room, she was upset not because I had been getting stoned since I was eight years old, but because I was smoking low-grade shake, and, from her perspective, paying too much for it. Her admonition: from then on, I was to smoke with her and her friends, and if I needed my own stash, I was to ask her for it.

I did.

From that point forward, my mother was the cool mom who let me and my friends use her tab at the local liquor store, who let us hang out and smoke weed as much as we wanted—and later, when I had access to better pot than she did, the tables turned and it was she who came to me when she needed a smoke. There were never limits with my mom, no real rules with regard to drugs or any other sort of behavior; even her admonition about acid and heroin was toothless, at best theoretical. In the absence of boundaries, I had nothing to push against, but in my adolescent way I needed a reaction of some kind—I needed to know that I could have an impact on something, anything. The summer after Reagan was elected, when I came home from boarding school I told my mother I was now a Republican—it was the only way I could think of to get a rise out of her, and indeed, I got a reaction. (For the record, I was not, nor have I ever been, a Republican; after Reagan's inauguration, my high school friends and I wore black armbands for a week.)

I recall going to a party at the age of thirteen or so, and asking my mother for some pot to take with me to my first real bash with the older, high school kids with whom I wanted to make an entrance. I showed up with a quarter ounce of good bud my mom had given me, handed it to someone, and proceeded to get obscenely drunk on Mickey's Big Mouth malt liquor. At home, I threw up all over myself and blacked out, awoke the next morning with my first real hangover and the humiliating realization that my mom had thrown me in the shower and cleaned up my mess.

She cleaned up a number of my messes, or at least tried. In boarding school I blacked out on alcohol yet again, woke up in the school infirmary, and was suspended; she tried to challenge the school, to clean up after me. But this time, I told her to leave it alone. I knew there was no way around my punishment, and happily spent the week of my suspension at my cousin Jane's house in Westport, swimming in her pool and eating takeout from Stew Leonard's. In this, and in every other mess, I knew that although my mother would never set a limit, she would always show up—as she did when I was in Phoenix House in New York, when each week she drove five hours each way from Massachusetts to attend family therapy.

I don't know what the result would have been had I been given more limits, clearer boundaries against which to butt my head. Perhaps I would have felt more secure, more contained; perhaps I would simply have become angrier and more rebellious than I already was. I know that I was enticed by the world of drugs, especially those that were "forbidden." My heroes were people like Iggy Pop, Hunter Thompson, Ken Kesey, Keith Richards, and William Burroughs. And I probably would have been drawn to them, and to that culture, regardless of any external pressure or lack thereof. I do know that being left to find my own limits drew me to depths I otherwise would not have reached, to a netherworld, whither there was nowhere to go but death, and which required me to seek ways to contain the alchemical process of transformation—to create boundaries in some form. Without externally imposed structure, the only possibility left me was to fall limitlessly into darkness, and, perhaps through some sort of grace, to enter an alembic, an alchemical vessel forged of necessity, even perhaps of choice. With regard to my upbringing, to the absence of structure inherent in my mother's judgment and my father's absence, I can only say that I remain incredulous, and that at the same time I am profoundly grateful.

Forgiveness, Oppression, and Grace

> *"Grace strikes us when we are in great pain
> and restlessness. It strikes us when we walk
> through the dark valley of a meaningless and
> empty life. It strikes us when we feel that our
> separation is deeper than usual, because we
> have violated another life, a life which we
> loved, or from which we were estranged."*
> —Paul Tillich

> *"It's a hell of a thing, killin' a man. Take away
> all he's got, and all he's ever gunna have."*
> —William Tunney in *Unforgiven*

As with my mother, my father's love for me
has never been in question, but there have
been times when it has felt less than loving. When
I was a small child he and I were very close, but
in subsequent years the emotional and geographic
distance grew between him and my mother, and
consequently he became more distant from me, too.
During my adolescence he spiraled into depression, and as he struggled with the after-effects of
a traumatic head injury suffered in a horrendous
car wreck, his alcoholism worsened; he began to
have blackouts of several days at a time, fueled by

rage and bourbon and the Xanax given him by an incompetent psychiatrist.

I was sixteen when I stopped him, in one of his blackouts, from throwing his girlfriend out of a window. We were at her condominium in Keaukaha—on the sixth floor, as I recall. I had sucked down a six-pack of Hamm's with dinner, and had prepared for sleep on the pullout couch in the living room. Half asleep, half drunk, I vaguely heard my father and his girlfriend having sex in the bedroom, and to those sounds I fell into a true sleep. I awoke, befuddled, to her screams, her pleas for him to stop.

I was in shock, had no idea how to respond; I hid under the covers and pretended to be asleep, still. I think my father's girlfriend called my name, asking for my help, and I remember my father, enraged, saying, "He's not coming, he's pretending to be asleep." As her pleas continued, and as I came more into awareness of what was happening, I couldn't continue to pretend—I went into the bedroom and saw my father roughly pushing his girlfriend toward the window. She had stopped struggling, and was now cowering, making herself small, trying to assuage his rage.

I grabbed my father by the shoulder, spun him around, and said, "That's enough." I didn't have to try very hard—he didn't resist when I stopped him. Perhaps he was simply hoping for some containment, for someone to refuse him the right of continued destruction, but at that moment, he was no longer larger than life for me, either figuratively or physically. It was at that moment that I knew I no longer had to be afraid of his rage, his unpredictability. I was bigger than he was, and he couldn't hurt me.

His girlfriend huddled, crying.

The next day my father was still drinking, still in a blackout. It was the weekend, and the three of us went from her condo to his house in Fern Forest—a remote area near the Volcano, accessible only by miles of dirt roads, where homes had outhouses and no electricity, where the neighbors were wild pigs and heavily armed pot growers. There my father continued to rage until finally, that afternoon, he fell asleep. I had been waiting; I packed my bag and walked the four miles to the highway.

I stood for a long time, thumb out, hoping for a ride. After a while, my father's girlfriend drove up in his truck; unable, unwilling to come himself, he'd sent her to bring me home. I told her it was she who should be following my lead, but she turned and drove back to my father, dutiful, afraid. I eventually got a ride with a man in a white Toyota pickup who owned a small antique store in the area; I know he knew something was wrong, but he was kind enough not to ask. He dropped me in Puna, at the home of a grower friend of my mother's, where I knew I'd find a meal, a joint to smoke, a couch to sleep on. It was harvest time, and huge plants were hanging from the rafters of the A-frame, drying, filling the house with the pungent smell of home.

My father has long since converted to Catholicism—a complex decision, and one I frankly still do not fully understand. Yet I suspect that at least a portion of his devotion to his new faith derives from a sincere sense of, to use the language of that faith, contrition, penitence. Though for many years he was medicated, drunk, out of his right mind, he's never made excuses, and in his actions since, in his relationship with me, in his dealings with the world, he has, in his own way, actively sought forgiveness. My father lives with his past, with the impact he's had on my life and on the lives of others; although he's never spoken of it, I know he remembers.

I, too, know how it feels to be ashamed, to have been out of control. I know how it feels to carry the responsibility for my behavior, but to wish it had been otherwise. I know how it feels to have fucked up, to have been powerless. I know how it feels to want, to need, to hope to be let off the hook. Yet, despite my empathy, despite my deep desire to do so, I have not yet been able to entirely forgive many experiences, many events: not my father, nor his father, nor his before him; not the Romans, the Catholics, the Cossacks, the Nazis; not the English for Ireland, the Turks for Armenia, the Seventh Cavalry for Wounded Knee.

Forgiveness, for the sake of both self and other, is offered in mainstream recovery, in psychotherapy, in spiritual practice. Fred Luskin's work on forgiveness is quite profound, and many others such as the Dalai Lama have written substantively on the freedom inherent in forgiveness, on the possibility of release for all involved—to paraphrase Paolo Freire, in freeing themselves from oppression, the oppressed also set free their oppressors, and from my perspective, lack of forgiveness is certainly among the worst forms of self-oppression. But the thing about forgiveness is that it can't be forced; it's really a kind of grace. I can want it, need it, wish for it; I can take steps toward it on many different paths. But fundamentally, it is not up to me—it is, ultimately, bestowed (or not), as Jung might have said, *deo concedente.*

FAITH AND FEAR

"Only one who has risked the fight with the dragon and is not overcome by it wins the hoard, the 'treasure hard to attain.' He alone has a genuine claim to self-confidence, for he has faced the dark ground of his self and thereby has gained himself. This experience gives him faith and trust, the pistis *in the ability of the self to sustain him, for everything that menaced him from inside he has made his own."*

—C. G. JUNG

"Only a man who knows what it is like to be defeated can reach down to the bottom of his soul and come up with the extra ounce of power it takes to win when the match is even."

—MUHAMMAD ALI

I grew up in a world in which the experience of fear was so pervasive that for many years I had no idea that life could be otherwise. In fear, the prevalent story is, "What's going to happen to me?" In mainstream recovery, this is often referred to as "self-centered" fear—fear that emerges from a kind of narcissistic self-involvement, from incomplete surrender. But at the root of this (understandable) fear-based preoccupation with outcome, with safety, is not simply a lack of surrender or a core story, but rather an experience of the body, the residue of which lies in shadow.

"Fear is lack of faith." The implication of this common expression is that if I have sufficient faith, I will no longer fear—and by inference, that if I am in fear I have somehow failed in faith, in my relationship to the divine. For me, this reinforces the idea that all fear is pathological, and the sense that I am somehow inadequate—that the presence of fear, the lack of sufficient faith, is due to my failure.

This tautology of blame simply doesn't work for me. It engages the erroneous belief that I should be elsewhere, different, away from what is here and now—a dangerous "should" that enacts my core shame, and that for me makes faith even more inaccessible. In desiring, even requiring a shift away from the important, uncomfortable experience of fear, this process re-enacts the very traumatic disconnection which is at the root of the fear in the first place.

There is, in my experience, a utility to fear—even to the extent that fear itself can be a source of faith. This brings to mind Kierkegaard's notion of fear and trembling—a way of relating to the divine that derives from the realities of being human, from the existential struggle with hopelessness, meaninglessness, isolation, disconnection. This non-traumatic fear, for me, is an appropriate response to the awesome vastness of being; to disengage with this aspect of human truth, this fundamental experience, to require a leap of faith as a "cure" for fear, becomes a kind of spiritual bypass—really, a form of denial, a disconnection from an important experience that, if entered into fully, can be profoundly fruitful.

The idea that fear is a lack of faith suggests an artificially binary reality—I am either in fear, or I am in faith—and for me this is lacking in nuance. As Jung suggests in his notion of *pistis*—the trusting heart—there is indeed an intermediate step between fear and faith, a process that cannot be bypassed: the development of trust through engagement with the darkest, most eschewed aspects of one's being. The disruption of energy, embodiment, and directionality so pervasive in the experience of trauma is, most essentially, an injury to the capacity for trust, but not simply a blind trust in the world itself, in caregivers, in the divine. It is, rather, trust in oneself, in one's subjective experience, in one's fundamental perceptions, found only in the willingness to enter into fear, to engage in the self-compassionate process of leaning in. The trust so important as a precursor to faith—and so essential for post-traumatic recovery—is, in my experience, not a leap. Rather, it is a capacity slow to develop, and one which requires acceptance of the natural ebb and flow of fear and faith, without the intent of being elsewhere.

In the experience of rupture, in the loss of embodiment and the disconnection from both personal and ancestral root, lies indeed a kind of self-centeredness, even of what psychologists call narcissistic injury. But in my experience (and in the work of Jungian analyst Mario Jacoby) the process of entering into this injury gives rise to reconnection, to conscious engagement with, in the words of Paul Tillich, the "ground of all being." Through going beneath the story of, "What's going to happen to me," through a deepening relationship with the injury in body and psyche, I learn to trust my most fundamental experience even—or perhaps especially—when that experience is fear.

MY MISSING GRANDMOTHER

*"We are volcanoes. When we women offer our
experience as our truth, as human truth, all
the maps change. There are new mountains."*
—URSULA K. LEGUIN

Most of what I know about my paternal grandmother is in the form of snippets, apocrypha,
and my own fantasy. In my father's youth, she seems
always to have been in the background—a presence,
yes, but a presence lost in the chaos of my paternal
grandfather's drama and destruction. My aunt, my
father's sister, refers to her mother as a saint, but
what I hear in that description of "sainthood" is a
lack of recourse—a resignation to a life of abuse,
trauma, and negation. I have a sense of my grandmother as having been kind and warm, but also of
her not having been allowed by her circumstances,
by her history, by her common-law husband, to have
her own being.

My grandmother's father left his home in Siberia
in 1916, leaving his wife and two daughters—my
grandmother and her sister. According to various stories, he either left in search of work and a better life
in the U.S., or he simply ran away, fleeing his family
and responsibilities—perhaps both. In any case, my

great grandmother and her two daughters left Omsk in 1917, in pursuit of my great grandfather. They came via Shanghai and San Francisco, and eventually arrived in New York, but they never found him.

It's not entirely clear how their forebears wound up in Siberia. Russian Jews were settled in Siberia during the nineteenth century; perhaps my grandmother's ancestors were among them. It's also possible that she was in part descended from the Krymchaks—Jews of the Crimea, of mixed Ashkenazic and Sephardic descent. I've heard both the family names Rosenberg and Rigosa, so it seems evident there was some intermixture of Central and Southern European Jews, but in looking at photographs of my grandmother, it's likely there was some Central Asian heritage as well—to my eyes, she looks decidedly Tatar.

Ultimately, though, I have no idea where her family came from, a fact that seems to me significant, even diagnostic of her apparent disappearance in her own life. What I do know, what I have heard, are stories from my father of his childhood: stories of his grandmother keeping live carp in the bathtub until she could cook them, fresh; stories of his family's poverty, of his father's chronic unemployment and violence; stories of anti-Semitism, of my father being chased home after school by gentile boys trying to hit him with sticks driven through at their ends with rusty nails. I've heard stories of his mother's kindness, of the special connection he had with her, of his gleeful sharing with her the forbidden *tref* of shrimp fried rice and other Chinese delicacies. I've heard stories of his sister's escape from the family insanity as early as she was able: at sixteen, she married a kind, decent man, and fled, much to her credit. And I've heard stories of the abuse my grandmother suffered at the hands of my grandfather—of my father's attempts, as a little boy, to rescue her, to insert himself in the violence, only to be thrown about as well.

When I think of my grandmother, what arises for me is an ongoing question: where was she? Aside from this person who was a saint, or a martyr, or the victim of abuse and oppression, or a wonderful loving mother, where *was* she? My grandmother was obese and diabetic; perhaps in her traumatization, in her inability to find alternate possibilities of life, she took comfort in food. Or perhaps she was simply self-destructive, enacting her history and that of her family on her own body. Probably both, but also, in my fantasy, is the possibility that this was the only way in which she could be known, in which she could have a presence—through her obesity, through her illness. But really, where was *she*, and was this condition—which ultimately killed her, when my father was fourteen—the result of feeling like she didn't have the right to anything better, to be heard, to exist, even to take up space in the world?

There are many gaps here, many holes, a great deal of conjecture. What I'm most aware of, what I feel most, is shame—a sense of not having the right to exist, of only being allowed to have presence, to be known, through self-destruction. I'm aware of my father carrying this particular form of shame, the legacy of his mother's inheritance from her own lineage, magnified in the trauma of her life with my grandfather, in her being lost in his utter insanity. I'm aware of my father having inherited from her this experience of not wanting to be, not feeling entitled to be—of living only in a kind of absent martyrdom. I'm aware of having inherited this from him, and from her—this core shame, this historical transmission so evocative of the remoteness of Siberia, so evident in the loss of lineage, in the disconnection of oppression and immigration and poverty. And I'm aware, in my deepest intuition, of some possibility of transformation for all of us in an embodied being, in the process of my finding presence in my life, in the world, in my own integrity—and in my ongoing, purposeful refusal to negate the most fundamental aspects of my own being.

My Kidney Pulse

"He whose eye happens to look down into the yawning abyss becomes dizzy. But what is the reason for this? It is just as much in his own eye as in the abyss, for suppose he had not looked down."
—Søren Kierkegaard

Kidney is water; it is the foundation of being. It is the embodied, energetic connection of personal and transpersonal, the link between that which exists above the surface and the primordial depths of the archetypal—the ancestral realm in which the past emerges in the fundament of the body.

Pulse diagnosis is a foundation of Chinese medicine, and in my kidney pulse (to be precise, the left *chi* position, at the deepest level) is a subtle hollowness—a hollowness that is at once an experience of this life, a somatic reality, and a story of my ancestors. An acupuncturist colleague described this emptiness in my kidney pulse as "uterine," meaning that it reflects the emergence of my mother's pregnancy in my body, my life—and it reflects an ancestral link, or what in Chinese medicine is referred to as prenatal *qi*. According to modern "traditional" Chinese medicine, which is relatively concrete in its

123

understanding of such things, prenatal *qi* is a sort
of DNA, a literal, physical inheritance of the traits
of ancestors—eye color, physical constitution, body
shape, and so on. However, from a more esoteric,
classical perspective, this phenomenon of prenatal
qi suggests a deeper layer of connection with an
intergenerational root, an energetic link not only
to physical lineage, but also a transmission of the
somatic-energetic-psychological experience of those
who came before.

My parents, recently married, were living in
Honolulu when my mother became pregnant with
me. According to the story I've been told, during her
pregnancy she began to spot, and sought consulta-
tion from local physicians—who, in the mid-1960s,
in Hawaii, were not widely known for their compe-
tence. These physicians told my parents that I would
be born retarded and deformed. My parents, in disbelief, almost immediately returned to New York,
where my father completed graduate school, and
where I was born, at Mount Sinai Hospital, after
my mother's water broke at a Horn and Hardart
automat in Midtown Manhattan—an image I've
always found somehow fitting.

My parents, I'm reasonably certain, were never
well suited for each other. At the very least, I don't
think my father ever wanted to leave Hawaii, and
I don't think my mother ever wanted to stay (or,
later, to return). They loved each other, at least in

the beginning of their relationship, but it's my sense that their love was based on an intensity of attraction, not on any real compatibility or shared reality; in my imagination, the hollowness of their connection is at least a part of what emerged in my gestation—and what is reflected in my kidney pulse. But this essential disconnection between my parents, reflected in my prenatal *qi*, is at the same time a physical and energetic connection with the ghostly emptiness of my ancestors' experience, with their deprivation, with a heritage of trauma.

The prenatal emptiness of my kidney pulse has always been a presence—or perhaps more accurately, an absence—in my postnatal life. In a sense, this experience of rootlessness is what set the stage for my lifelong struggle with simply being alive, being in the world, and which (of course) emerged for a time in my profound affection for heroin. Although it never actually filled that empty space, heroin allowed me to tolerate the void without feeling constantly like I would fall in.

As Jung said, every complex formed of human experience has an archetypal core; in my understanding of kidney in Chinese medicine, the emptiness activated in my prenatal experience is the place at which personal and transpersonal interact. In a sense, this void is the phenomenon that sets the stage for my experience of traumatic disconnection in postnatal life; if there is such thing as a "genetic" predisposition for addiction, this is its energetic underpinning. And at the same time, emptiness is also an essential aspect of human being—the embodied experience of existential anxiety in response to the ultimate inescapability of non-being. In some sense, an awareness that this experience is shared with humanity at large allows me to be with, even welcome, this root of my life, and of life in the human realm—this root which draws together in my body the disparate threads of my parents' reality, my ancestral heritage, my life as an addict, and the ground of all being. In the kidney, this interplay of prenatal and postnatal, personal and transpersonal, individual and universal, presents a possibility of transformation for all of these levels of experience, and at the same time is an embodied connection with the ordinary reality of being human.

RECOVERY PROGRAM, PROGRAM OF RECOVERY

"The first step toward finding God, Who is Truth, is to discover the truth about myself: and if I have been in error, this first step to truth is the discovery of my error."
—THOMAS MERTON

"They were gonna make me a major for this, and I wasn't even in their fuckin' army any more."
—CAPTAIN WILLARD, *Apocalypse Now*

I grew up feeling isolated, disconnected, alone, feeling as if no one could understand my condition—feelings, of course, shared by many addicts. For me, in part, this youthful experience was a very real consequence of being an intellectual, introverted Jew growing up in a rural community in Hawaii, in which one was either a *Haole* or a Local, and in which I was effectively neither. In part this was also the result of my chaotic family life, and of the withdrawal that was my self-protective response. And, admittedly, it's to some extent my nature to be existentially preoccupied, to be more focused on the experience of alienation and the struggle for meaning as a human being than, say, baseball.

At any rate, as is often the case, over the course of my active addiction I became increasingly isolated. I had friends, associates, but I felt increasingly alone, increasingly as if I didn't belong in the world, increasingly worthless, ashamed, undeserving of human interaction and affection.

Phoenix House was the first time in my memory that I felt as if I belonged. I was welcomed; I felt connected. I felt as if my experience, shared by others, was now the foundation of a bond, a community, even a family. Along with this experience came a form of behavior modification characterized by intense confrontation, hard and fast rules with swift and severe consequences, black and white perceptions, rigid ideas and expectations. But early on I desperately needed this kind of approach—I was so disconnected from myself I needed an externally imposed structure, a structure of rigid accountability, simply in order to survive and not self-destruct.

After treatment, in mainstream recovery, I found another wonderful community, a deep and substantive means of transformation, but also, in many instances, a rigidity of thought and belief verging on religious fundamentalism. I often encountered the critical, judgmental aspect of this world—an ideology that insisted that there was a right and a wrong way to be in recovery, that there was a recovery that was "with the program," and that anything else put one outside the fold.

There was a point at which something shifted for me—a point at which it became essential for me to differentiate between a recovery program and a program of recovery, at which it became essential that my own perceptions and internal sense of integrity took precedence over external structures and ideologies. It was at this point that I began, so to speak, to go off the reservation. From a mainstream recovery perspective, this might be perceived as self-willed, insufficiently surrendered, even, perhaps, as a manifestation of my "disease." But to be clear, it was not that mainstream recovery lost value; in fact, quite the contrary—my divergence allowed for me a deepening of my engagement with the substantive aspects of mainstream recovery, a deepening connection with my own subtle process. It was, simply, that at that point of transition, engaging in recovery according to someone else's idea of what that meant had the effect of intensifying the experience of disconnection from my own vitality that had set the stage for my addiction in the first place. In fact, it was the very things that I had learned, the things that I had internalized through the process of early recovery, that not only allowed me to prioritize my own perceptions over those of a recovery program—they made it imperative for me to do so.

In Chinese medicine, thought is associated with the earth element—the spleen and stomach, also responsible for the parallel process of digestion.

Rigidity of thought, rumination, obsessional thinking—all of which are, of course, components of
active addiction—are a disorder of the spleen, but
a disorder with the potential to go deep into psyche
and soma. According to Master Jeffrey Yuen, rigid
patterns of thought create stagnation of *qi*, which
eventually, in turn, creates stagnation of blood.
These conditions are in and of themselves problematic, but are even more destructive in the way in
which they generate heat and phlegm, penetrating
the deepest layers of the body and causing myriad
diseases, both physical and psychological.

From at least one Daoist perspective, fixedness
is in and of itself a kind of illness. From a more
medical sense, fixedness is an illness that cannot be
addressed by the imposition of more fixed ideas, ideologies, and external structures, but rather only by
the development of fluidity in body and mind. These
qualities, ultimately, derive from following the often-
unpredictable sense of what truly feels right—from
developing the kind of personal, visceral, energetic
connection I've sought to describe—rather than
adhering to ideologies that promise some form of
predictable outcome, ideologies that are rooted in
the avoidance of fear rather than acceptance of the
radical contingency of human life.

Addiction is essentially a form of rigidity—rigidity of thought, of behavior, of patterns of every
kind. It is a kind of pathological fixedness of both

self-perception and being-in-the-world. It is a profound immobilization characterized by black and white thinking, obsession, utter spiritual, psychological, and behavioral constriction—a stuckness that only changes with the recognition that one is stuck, and the recognition that on one's own one lacks the capacity to become unstuck.

This concept is profound, and like the other concepts and principles of mainstream recovery, when held lightly it can be utterly transformative. But when adhered to rigidly, religiously, these concepts generate not only a kind of fundamentalist, authoritarian ideology but also a rigidity of thought that becomes self-defining, self-fulfilling, and, perhaps most damning, self-limiting. This kind of tautology is destructive—first, in the sense that it constricts the possibility of a fluid way of being that is consistent with full engagement in the human experience, and also in a deeply energetic, even physiological sense: rigidity of thought, belief, and ideology are in and of themselves a kind of disease, and if in fact addiction is a disease, this secondary disease of rigidity is not a form of recovery, but rather is yet another manifestation of the original illness.

OLD WOUNDS

*"Either way, change will come. It could be
bloody, or it could be beautiful. It depends
on us."*

—ARUNDHATI ROY

The first memory I have is of a wound. I was
four, I think. We lived on Grosvenor Avenue in
Fieldston, an exclusive area within Riverdale, in the
Bronx, in an old house in which the previous owner,
Mr. Bach, had died. My parents joked about the
ghost of Mr. Bach living in the house with us and
our pets: a cat named Boris, and our collie, Pokey.

My memories of that house, of that neighborhood,
are in snapshots, impressions: the smell and feel of a
navy surplus blanket with which I slept every night;
a cage full of pet scorpions left with my parents by
some friends while they went to Morocco; an iguana
named Tootsie; my grandparents' Saturday visits.

There was a vacant lot full of trees next to our
house, a lot my neighborhood friends and I called
"the woods." We played there, or in the street, which
was safe, devoid of all but the minimal local traffic—
we played street hockey in the summer, and skated on
the nearby pond in the winter. Carly Simon—before
she was *Carly Simon*—lived up the street, with her

mother and sisters; she babysat me once or twice, a fact which my mother made sure to tell and retell at every opportunity. This being the late '60s, my mother's outfits were a bit wild, colorful, flowing; I recall the old Saab she drove, and the smell of saffron rice with shrimp, her best dish, coming from the kitchen. I had watered wine at dinner, which I loved.

My father was finishing his Ph.D. at Columbia, teaching at Lehman College, working as an assistant curator at The Met—all, I think, in order to keep up this lifestyle in a home in a neighborhood my parents really couldn't afford. I recall feeling his presence in the house in a way which was absent later in my life; I recall his study, full of his smells of bourbon and Between the Acts, the little cigars he smoked constantly. He worked on the house, too, repairing the constant flow of things going wrong in the old ramshackle place. He painted the floor, white with grey trim, or perhaps the other way around. Friends of my parents would often come by—sculptors and painters who were then or who would later become famous. For me, they were just babysitters and companions.

I remember hot chocolate on the front steps in the winter.

But my first linear, narrative memory is of a wound. My mother, an artist, worked in a variety of media, one of which was wood and linoleum block prints, for which she used a set of small, grooved chisels. One day she gave me the chisels and a block of balsa wood to carve, left me in her upstairs bedroom to play, and went downstairs to the kitchen, to prepare dinner, perhaps. I remember the look of the chisels, the feel and lightness of the balsa wood, my desire to make a long slice through it—and I remember the movement of the chisel as I held the wood in my left hand, raised the chisel high in my right, and swung downwards toward the block. I remember the shock as the little knife glanced off the wood and sliced clean through my hand, along my forefinger and down into the palm. I remember the open wound, seeing white bone and sinew, then starting to bleed, then starting to scream.

It took a while for my mother to hear me. It seemed like forever. She came running upstairs, took me in her arms, and amidst blood and tears carried me to the foyer. Among all those vivid memories, one of the most vivid is seeing, over my mother's shoulder as she carried me down the stairs, droplets of my blood on the newly painted floor. I remember feeling terrible because my father, I thought, would have to repaint the floor.

I was taken to the hospital, where my mother insisted on a consult from the neurosurgeon husband of her friend Marlene, evincing concern that my special little hand remain special, concern that had been absent when leaving her four-year-old child with sharp tools and a block of wood, because somehow, in her need for me to be special, to be remarkable, she thought I could handle anything.

I recall the excruciating pain of the wound being irrigated, the doctor and the nurses kindly holding me while I screamed, while he stitched—pain, I think, worse than the initial gash, as the pain of healing, of reparation often is. And later, when at least the fleshly part of the wound healed, I took pride in having had seven stitches, which for me, at that age, seemed a great many. I took great pride in my lifelong scar.

Connection
and Disconnection

"Concepts, like individuals, have their histories and are just as incapable of withstanding the ravages of time as are individuals. But in and through all this they retain a kind of homesickness for the scenes of their childhood."
— Søren Kierkegaard

My father was on his own after his parents died; he was fourteen. His older brother and sister had long since fled the utter insanity of their father's violence, and my father's paternal uncle, Robert, a physical education teacher in the New York City public schools, refused to take my father in. My dad was very close to his first cousin Sam, Robert's son, but Robert's psychoanalyst told him the relationship between the two boys was destructive, so Robert elected to leave his barely-teenage nephew to fend for himself.

I'm not sure how my dad survived, but he did. At some point he became the superintendent of a tenement, somewhere in the Bronx or upper Manhattan, and as the super he was given an apartment. He worked in a pet shop, I think, and at a library, and went to the High School for the Visual Arts—the sister school of the performing arts high school memorialized in the movie *Fame*.

My father had grown up in some degree of orthodoxy, but as a teenager, after his parents died, left that framework behind—out of necessity, out of grief, in simple distaste, or perhaps all of the above. At some point he was at a luncheonette, he once told me, eating a hamburger, and he ordered an egg cream—a New York favorite, milk, seltzer, and chocolate syrup—which he drank with his burger. He realized, suddenly, that he had for the first time combined milk and meat, had violated a precept with which he'd been indoctrinated from birth. He ran out into the street and threw up from the shock of it—from the existential crisis inherent in the beginnings of an unorthodox life.

I'm not sure at what point my father started to drink. He and his friend Ritt, later a well-known sculptor, were known for their drunken escapades. A talented visual artist, my father was by nature more inclined in the direction of academia, art history, than he was studio art; before college, at age nineteen, he became art editor for *Dance* magazine—a job from which he was fired for some inappropriate behavior, perhaps a fistfight, related to his drinking. From there he enrolled at Hunter, one of the colleges of the City University of New York.

My mother was, in many ways, a stereotypical daddy's girl. Her father doted on her—or, at least, was kind to her, even if he didn't understand her, in contradistinction to her mother's judgment and criticism. Blue collar though her family was, my mother was given a sports car when she was sixteen, which she promptly wrecked. She was rescued from consequences by my grandfather.

She was talented, my mother—unconventional, even brilliant. She won an award in high school—a Bausch and Lomb science award, or something of the sort, that would have paid for college, possibly even medical school. But in her conservative family, girls didn't go to college—my grandmother had wanted to go to college, but wasn't allowed; consequently, neither was my mother. My mother was beautiful, even striking, so rather than being allowed to manifest her own talent, she was sent to school to become a medical technician—so she could work in a hospital, so she could meet and marry a wealthy physician, because that was what pretty girls did.

She acquiesced—she attended medical technician school, and had a hospital job, at least for a while. But although my mother's unconventionality has in many ways been a source of pain, of a variety of problems for her—and for me—in this instance it saved her: she fled the structured life of Bayside and, this being the early 1960s, started listening to Bob Dylan and Joan Baez, started hanging around in the West Village, and eventually went to Hunter College, despite her parents' open disapproval.

My parents met at Hunter, of course. One day in class, my mother, a junior, brought my father, a senior, a cup of coffee. When my father left for graduate school at the East West Center at the University of Hawaii, my mother followed, and they were married shortly thereafter.

I always heard these stories of my parents' lives in allusion, in drunken asides, or in terse responses to my occasional inquiries. I'm not sure how much of my memory is accurate—how much is fantasy, how much is apocryphal, how much is my own emphasis on certain details that, in light of my own stories, stand out for me. I was always aware, I think, of my parents' wounds, and certainly of their disconnection from each other—even when I was small, when we lived in Riverdale, I remember distance, fights, emptiness, a kind of vacuous realm in that big old house. But it wasn't as if I was consciously aware. I knew, but didn't know, in the spirit of Christopher Bollas' unthought known—in the same way in which my parents, until the end of their marriage, didn't let themselves know that whatever it was they shared was, fundamentally, broken.

Independently and with each other, in their post-divorce lives and subsequent relationships, my parents have for much of their lives been products of their disconnection, of the legacy of their families, their histories, the traumatized Judaism from which they came, and the fragmented culture in which they came to adulthood. Neither was ever allowed, ever given permission, to value their own perceptions, their own desires. In some ways, though, it wasn't an experience of being "allowed" as much as it was a life of never having known any other possibility, of not having a context for imagining something else. Their families, in their disconnection, in their own legacy of trauma, had no concept of what it was they carried—what it was they lacked. Later in life—much later—my parents both came to know themselves differently, to in some way manifest something authentic, but this was only after years of wreckage and destruction, after years of alcohol and drugs and violence and chaos. In the meantime, as it was for my parents, disconnection was the energetic fabric of my upbringing, the matrix out of which my psyche formed—a matrix with roots extending into the distant past of oppression and brutality, with a trunk emerging from immigration and economic survival and cultural fragmentation, with branches and leaves steeped in alcohol and cocaine, and, for me, once upon a time, in the warm blanket of the opiate embrace.

CONCLUSION

"The only dream worth having is to dream that you will live while you are alive, and die only when you are dead. To love, to be loved. To never forget your own insignificance. To never get used to the unspeakable violence and vulgar disparity of the life around you. To seek joy in the saddest places. To pursue beauty to its lair. To never simplify what is complicated or complicate what is simple. To respect strength, never power. Above all to watch. To try and understand. To never look away. And never, never to forget."
—ARUNDHATI ROY

The process of writing this book, *The Trusting Heart*, has been transformative for me. It has been exactly that of which I write: the practice of connecting with my own energy, my stories, my intuition, my subjectivity, and allowing them to take me wherever they may lead, regardless of what might make "sense," what might be a desirable outcome.

As a result, this work is, perhaps, a bit meandering. To some extent, this is simply an artifact of the material, and of how it emerged from psyche; to some extent this is purposeful—an intentional reflection of Jung's idea of circumambulation of the psyche.

With the exception of referring here and there to methods of healing and inquiry which have been helpful for me, I have purposefully not offered "solutions" for the phenomena of addiction, trauma, intergenerational or ancestral trauma, and disconnection of various kinds. In *Recommended Reading* I do note some texts that have been meaningful for me, but, fundamentally, this book is not about practical interventions nor methods; it is about following an intuitive, deeply felt process rather than adhering to any externally structured methods, goals, techniques, or agendas. As such, it is my hope that each person find that which is true for them, that each person learn to engage with, to follow, to give credence and legitimacy to their own red thread. Ultimately, it is that which I hope this book will evoke—that in the deepest forms of resonance, in the process of giving ourselves permission to reconnect with what is most authentic for us, we develop that most essential quality of *pistis*: the trusting heart.

Recommended Reading

Samuels, Andrew, et al. *A Critical Dictionary of Jungian Analysis.*

Jaffe, Aniela. *The Myth of Meaning.*

Trungpa, Chogyam. *Cutting Through Spiritual Materialism.*

Grof, Christina. *The Thirst for Wholeness.*

Jung, C. G. *Memories, Dreams, Reflections.*

Duran, Eduardo. *Buddha in Redface.*

————. *Healing the Soul Wound.*

Wiesel, Elie. *Souls on Fire.*

Becker, Ernest. *Denial of Death.*

Bayda, Ezra. *At Home in the Muddy Water.*

Mate, Gabor. *In the Realm of Hungry Ghosts.*

Neff, Kristin. *Self-Compassion.*

Dechar, Lori Eve. *Five Spirits.*

Levine, Noah. *Dharma Punx.*

Tillich, Paul. *The Courage to Be.*

Watzlawick, Paul. *The Situation is Hopeless but Not Serious.*

Chödrön, Pema. *Taking the Leap.*

————. *When Things Fall Apart.*

Levine, Peter. *Taming the Tiger.*

Brach, Tara. *Radical Acceptance.*